re'. Remember.... Never forget. There

זכור לא... תשכח חריתך

te... Nunka te olvides. Hay esper

צן פאראן האפענונג פ

ope for your future. Remember... Neve

זור לאחריתך זכור לא... תשכח ויש

Akodrate... Nunka te olvides.

סן פאראן האפענונג פאר דיין צוה

forget. There is hope for your future.

זכור לא... תשכח ויש תקוה לאחרי

para tu postremeria. Akodrate... N

פאר דיין צוקונפט געדענק... קיין

Remember... Never forget. There is hop

שכח ויש תקוה לאחריתך זכור לא

es. Hay esperansa para tu postreme

TO LIFE

36 Stories of Memory and Hope

MUSEUM OF JEWISH HERITAGE
A LIVING MEMORIAL TO THE HOLOCAUST

Photographs gathered by the Association of Sons and Daughters of Jews Deported from France and by Serge and Beate Klarsfeld as installed at the Museum of Jewish Heritage—A Living Memorial to the Holocaust. Jews deported from France are shown at the Museum not as they died, but as they lived—a gesture of respect to the victims and their families, and a gesture of defiance to the Nazis, who attempted to obliterate their memory.

To Life

36 Stories of Memory and Hope

MUSEUM OF JEWISH HERITAGE
A LIVING MEMORIAL TO THE HOLOCAUST

Foreword by Robert M. Morgenthau

Preface and historical essay by David G. Marwell, Ph.D.

BULFINCH PRESS
AOL Time Warner Book Group
Boston · New York · London

MUSEUM OF JEWISH HERITAGE

A LIVING MEMORIAL TO THE HOLOCAUST

18 First Place

New York, NY 10280

www.mjhnyc.org

Project Director: Ivy L. Barsky

Project Manager: Ilana Abramovitch, Ph.D.

Project Coordinator: Tracy J. Figueroa

COMMITTEE

Rina Goldberg

Louis D. Levine, Ph.D.

Yitzchak Mais

David G. Marwell, Ph.D.

Design by Jerry Kelly

Photography by Richard P. Goodbody, Inc.

FIRST EDITION

ISBN 0-8212-2773-4

LCCN 2002102358

Bulfinch Press is a division of AOL Time Warner Book Group.

PRINTED IN SINGAPORE

Remember . . . never forget

Deuteronomy 25:17, 19

There is hope for your future

Jeremiah 31:17

This book is dedicated to Sally and Abe Magid, in celebration of more than fifty years of marriage, and to their children and their children's families. *To Life: 36 Stories of Memory and Hope* is an important complement to the message of the Museum, and it is our hope that this book will inspire future generations.

Lawrence and Millie Magid · *Alfred, Melissa, David, Jordan*
Harold and Rhonda Magid · *Emily, Julia, Lilly*
Richard and Carol Ann Magid · *Jessica, Risa*
Marc and Amy Magid · *Zachary, Samson*

Contents

Photo by David Sundberg

FOREWORD

Among institutions of Holocaust remembrance, the Museum of Jewish Heritage—A Living Memorial to the Holocaust, in New York City, is exceptional. Its history began in 1947, with the placement of an engraved stone in Riverside Park that reads: "This is the site for the American memorial to the heroes of the Warsaw Ghetto battle April–May 1943 and to the 6 million Jews of Europe martyred in the cause of human liberty." The Museum itself, a good five miles south of that original monument, stands as a testament to the lives that were lost during the Holocaust and to the lives that were rebuilt after the end of World War II.

More than thirty years later, Mayor Edward I. Koch attended a ceremony honoring the memory of those who died in the Holocaust. At the event, organized by the Warsaw Ghetto Resistance Organization, Mayor Koch noted that although this ceremony was held annually, each year there were fewer and fewer survivors in attendance, and he wondered if in his lifetime there might be no one left to relate their stories. Mayor Koch created a Holocaust task force whose work determined that a museum and a memorial should be built in New York City. The New York Holocaust Commission was established in 1982, and shortly thereafter, the State of New York offered land, proposing that the Museum be constructed at the southernmost tip of Manhattan, a site in geographic dialogue with such distinct American landmarks as the Statue of Liberty and Ellis Island.

Who could refuse an offer like this?

We began to build the staff, to collect artifacts, photographs, and audio and video testimony. As one of the repositories of Steven Spielberg's Survivors of the Shoah Visual History Foundation, we were able to give voice and breath to these histories. All of these efforts were supported by the tireless cochairmen—George Klein, Manfred Ohrenstein, and Howard J. Rubenstein, and by a dedicated Board of Trustees. Together we weathered the ups and downs of the financial climate of

New York City and, with a talented staff, built relationships over time with Holocaust survivors and their families. These people shared with us their precious memories and generously gave us the materials that allow us to tell their stories.

From the outset, we knew it was important to put the Holocaust in the context of Jewish life in the twentieth century—to show the lives and traditions that define Jewish life and allow Jewish culture to thrive. We wanted to illustrate that vibrant Jewish communities existed prior to the Holocaust. We endeavored to tell the story of the Holocaust using the voices of Jewish experience, to show that the victims of the Holocaust were not faceless or nameless. We sought to describe the renewal of Jewish life after the Shoah. Every object—every photograph, document, article of clothing, musical instrument, or candlestick—has a human story to transmit. It may be the story of a journey taken across an ocean to an unknown world, or the fond memories of a wedding attended in a shtetl. Or it may express a simple act of friendship during an icy winter in a labor camp. These objects represent lives lived and are witnesses to lives lost.

This focus on life is what makes the Museum of Jewish Heritage—A Living Memorial to the Holocaust distinct as a Holocaust memorial and a history museum. The Museum's doors opened in September 1997, and since that first day, visitors have said to us, "Here I really feel what was lost. I can appreciate these people. They were like my grandparents." And perhaps more important, these visitors have told us, "I want to take this experience home; I want to share it with people in my life who are important to me."

And that is why you hold this book in your hands.

The Museum's founding director, Dr. David Altshuler, who guided the Museum from 1986 to 1999, provided the book's genesis. He understood that the objects in the Museum, as well as the stories they tell, resonate for people long after the visit to the exhibition ends. This book is one way for the stories to be told again. Fortunately, Abe and Sally Magid understood this as well, and helped make the project a reality.

The Museum is organized into three chronological, thematic floors. "Jewish Life a Century Ago" explores the richness of Jewish culture with exhibits of life-cycle events, traditions and rituals, and daily life from the late-nineteenth century to the early 1930s. Visitors experience a portrait of the vibrant, diverse Jewish cul-

Torah scroll. Domazlice, Czechoslovakia. On permanent loan from the Memorial Scrolls Trust. This Torah was part of a vast collection of Jewish property looted by the Nazis. It was to be displayed in Prague in a museum of the "extinct Jewish race." Crafted according to ancient tradition, defiled by the Nazis, this Torah is cherished today as a symbol of Jewish heritage, survival, and Jewish renewal. In the background, three-dimensional images (PHSCologram Art Series produced by (ART)^n Laboratory) portray objects in the Museum's exhibition of Jewish life before, during, and after the Holocaust. Photo credit: Judy Davis/ Hoachlander Davis Photography.

ture that thrived in Europe and around the globe prior to World War II.

"The War Against the Jews" chronicles the years leading up to and including the Holocaust. After viewing an exhibit of the vital civilization and culture of the Jews on the first floor, visitors encounter Nazism's attempts to extinguish a culture and a people. The Museum focuses on illustrating the Jewish people's humanity, dignity, and spiritual resistance when confronted with the threat of extinction.

"Jewish Renewal" highlights the postwar years through the present. It illustrates the strength and vitality of the Jewish people and the revitalization of a civilization. It addresses Jewish response, on a global scale, to social injustice and intolerance after World War II. The exhibits ask the questions: What have we learned? and How can we be better to each other?

The Museum as a whole tells the story of what happens when government abuses its power and its citizens, and when laws are established to destroy people rather than to protect them. It illustrates the spiritual resistance that allowed the Jewish people to live and to go on to repair the community and the world at large.

We are a young and vital institution at the dawn of the twenty-first century. As we look toward the future and the expansion of the Museum and its educational mission, we know that just as the Jewish people have survived for millennia, the artifacts, testimony, and photographs that tell their stories must be preserved for generations to come.

Robert M. Morgenthau, *Chairman*

PREFACE

As you sit down to read this book and pore over the photographs, you may find yourself envisioning another era—a recollection that you have experienced a moment like this before. For many readers, the memory may be real or imagined, but it is an experience that builds bridges between generations. It is that moment when a grandparent takes down the family scrapbook and sits with an arm around you to introduce you to a part of the family you do not know.

People who look a little familiar peer out at you from yellowed photographs, smiling perhaps, holding flowers, or standing stiffly but honorably, wearing a soldier's uniform. You see these people, and maybe you smile back, but one thing is certain: their life experiences are important enough to be told to you again and again, so that you will remember, and your children will remember, and these relatives and family friends will never be forgotten.

Contained in this book are 36 stories of people who could be the grandparents, aunts, uncles, and parents of each of us—each person with a story to tell. The mere existence of these stories is a revelation, a miracle, and a blessed memory. They evoke other places and times. For some families, the stories that you read in this book are the only surviving remnants of their history.

And that is why these stories must be told.

These are personal recollections of 36 individuals. And while this book is by no means encyclopedic, we have tried to represent the diversity of experience and geography in the period we cover. These are the stories of hidden children, partisans, survivors of concentration camps and death camps, liberators, and Zionists, among others. Ordinary people whose choices and deeds in extraordinary times prove them to be truly remarkable human beings.

This is a book of memory, not a book of history. Individual memories flesh out the details, animating historical narrative with human drama. They illuminate the spaces where individual, family, and community intersect with the larger currents of political events. Powerful memories tell us how creative resourcefulness and untapped strength are mobilized in times of need.

The materials in this book represent just a fraction of the more than fifteen thousand objects in the Museum's collection. And from these we chose 36. Why 36 stories, as opposed to two dozen or four? The title, *36 Stories,* resonates for its numerological significance. In Hebrew, every letter also possesses a number value. *Chai,* whose value is 18, is the Hebrew word for life. It also carries the message of good luck and is known to many in the traditional toast, *l'chaim*—"To life!" Twice 18 equals 36, doubling the affirmation.

There is another explanation, less familiar, that also may be evoked in *36 Stories.*

It begins with a statement by a fourth-century Babylonian Jewish teacher, the first known to endow the number 36 with special significance in Jewish tradition. "The world is never without 36 just men," wrote the scholar known as Abbaye, "who daily receive the Divine Countenance." By the Middle Ages, 36 had become the most popular number in the kabbalah, or Jewish mysticism.

Hebrew- and Yiddish-speaking Jews invented a term for these 36 righteous individuals on whose merit the world exists—the lamed-vav, based on the Hebrew numeral for 36. Over time, the 36 righteous, or lamed-vavniks, had also taken on an additional characteristic—they had become hidden. In Jewish lore, stories were told of the lamed-vavniks radiating a righteousness that becomes increasingly important for the salvation of the world. But the 36 may be hidden even to themselves, and not know their own power. They are morally upright, but humble.

The 36 stories contained in this book take on added meaning in symbolizing the breadth and depth of Jewish life in the twentieth century. In 1986, the Museum began amassing documents, photographs, artifacts, home movies, and documentary film footage, along with audio and video testimony. These collections continue to expand today. Holocaust survivors and their families, as well as liberators, immigrants, and their families, donate these materials so that the Museum can fulfill its mission of educating future generations about Jewish life and the Holocaust. These materials are collected with a specific goal in mind—to show how Jews lived and how they live, not only how they died. The Museum has an unwavering commitment to commemorate the lives of those who perished as it honors those who struggled to survive to rebuild their lives, families, and communities.

The Hebrew word *za'chor* means "to remember." It appears in significant points in the Hebrew Bible, and it is a guiding principle, essential to the Museum's mission. One of the quotes that is installed on the frontispiece of the Museum's exhibition says: "Remember . . . never forget" *(Za'chor . . . lo tishkach).*

The Museum's interpretive strategy in our core exhibition is to relate personal stories through the display of objects and testimony. Creating a book of visual memories that similarly pairs objects and personal histories presents certain challenges, even though the Museum is fortunate to count among its family thousands of survivors. We could gather information only from those who survived, and we could include in the book only those who had managed, somehow, to keep an object that told their story. Yet there are no artifacts to represent certain memories visually—of clandestine worship, of the sharing of a priceless piece of bread, or of otherwise mundane acts of kindness in the face of evil. Many of these poignant stories—at least 6 million of them—cannot be illustrated in this book.

It is surely impossible to reduce the Museum experience, or indeed the history of the Holocaust and the years surrounding it, to 36 representative stories. But it is possible to "meet" these 36 people, to bring them home, and to introduce them to your family. Please read the stories; tell them to your children and grandchildren. Perhaps in doing so, we will emulate the righteous work of the lamed-vav.

David G. Marwell, Ph.D., *Director*

TO LIFE

36 Stories of Memory and Hope

MUSEUM OF JEWISH HERITAGE
A LIVING MEMORIAL TO THE HOLOCAUST

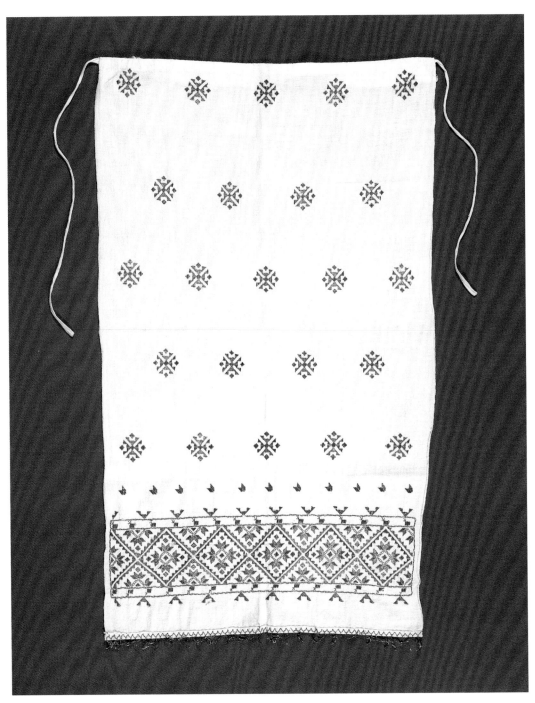

TROUSSEAU APRON

Embroidered apron made for the trousseau of Bella Grubstein, Letichev, Podolia. Ukraine, Russian Empire, 1909. Gift of Sonya Trachtenberg Breidbart. At age sixteen, Bella Grubstein was orphaned and began to run her family's foundry and furniture business. At twenty-six, she married Elya Trachtenberg, a Jewish communal leader and grain merchant.

Bella Trachtenberg
Bella

More than 2 million Russian and other eastern European Jewish immigrants, among them Bella and Elya Trachtenberg, arrived on America's shores in the decades between the 1880s and the early 1920s. The two main forces propelling their journey were a pervasive anti-Semitism at home and the dream of religious liberty and economic mobility in America.

Although most immigrants arrived poor and eventually improved their lives, often dramatically, America was not the *goldene medine* (the golden land) for everyone. For some, such as the Trachtenbergs, the adjustment proved extremely difficult.

Bella (Beyla) Grubstein was born in Letichev, a province of Podolia, in the Ukraine (Russian Empire) in 1883. The Letichev District was the birthplace of the Hasidic movement and the home of many distinguished rabbis. It was also an area that had its share of severe hardships and pogroms—government-inspired violent attacks on Jews. Orphaned at age sixteen, Bella was the oldest of six children and took on the responsibility of running her parents' businesses—an iron foundry and a furniture business. The youngest child was only two years old when Bella took over family responsibilities, but Bella was a young woman of determination, and eventually her devotion to family and work paid off. Using her excellent mathematical skills, she made her enterprises thrive, and then succeeded in putting her three brothers through medical school, two in Russia and one in Liège, Belgium.

When Bella Grubstein was twenty-six, she married Elya Trachtenberg, son of a wealthy family in Letichev. Although he did not need to, Elya worked in his family's grain business. He was also a leader in and an advocate for the Jewish community in Letichev—a job that, at that time, was not easy to fulfill.

After a civil war broke out in the former Russian Empire in 1918, the chaos and

Photograph of Bella Grubstein Trachtenberg and daughter, Milya Trachtenberg, in Letichev, Podolia. Ukraine, Russian Empire, circa 1915. Gift of Sonya Trachtenberg Breidbart.

attacks on the Jewish communities led many young people to consider immigration to Palestine or the New World as the only hope for a secure future. When the Trachtenbergs had their second daughter, Sonya, in 1921, they discussed the possibility of leaving for America, where two of Elya's younger brothers had already established themselves. (The Communists had already taken the Trachtenberg family business away.) Bella was opposed to leaving her hometown and her siblings, who were like children to her. She knew it would be best for her own children, but feared she would never see her brothers and sisters again. In 1922, after due consideration, the family made the painful decision to leave for America, and Bella never set eyes on her siblings again.

For a man such as Elya Trachtenberg, already forty-five years old, adjustment to the new language and the new culture in the United States proved difficult. In the beginning, he had a hard time finding work. Eventually, he sold life insurance and printing labels, but the family spent many years struggling against poverty. Even into his late fifties, the only work the charming and sociable Elya could get was sweeping floors for the Work Projects Administration.

However, before Bella and Elya Trachtenberg died in 1959 and 1965, respectively, they were able to see their grandchildren on their way to becoming actors in the American dream. Bella Grubstein Trachtenberg's talent with numbers was passed down to her children and grandchildren, who have excelled as mathematicians, one becoming a physician as well.

Rose Stavisker Fischman

Shabbat Shalom

In an era when women had few opportunities to pursue in higher education, Rose Stavisker's place in Columbia University's dental school class of 1905 was a distinguished achievement. Along with six others, she was about to be among the first women to graduate from a professional dentistry school in New York State. And yet she was prepared to sacrifice that achievement—or certainly defer it—if it forced her to violate her religious beliefs.

In 1905, final examinations at Columbia University's School of Dental and Oral Surgery were scheduled for a Saturday. That presented a serious problem for Rose Stavisker. As an Orthodox Jew, she could not write the examination on the Sabbath. She asked the school administration if she could take the examination on another date, but the school refused. Her only recourse was to wait another year until the final examinations of 1906, hoping that they would not again fall on a Saturday.

But that was not to be the end of the story.

Rose Stavisker was born in Poland in 1883 to Moses Stavisky and Hannah Greenberg. Her family immigrated to New York in 1887 and lived on Rivington Street in

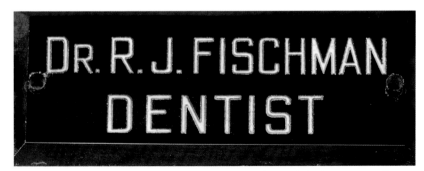

Plaque of Dr. Rose Fischman. Gold lettering on black, beveled edges. New York City, 1927–1941. Gift of Bernard D. Fischman in memory of Rose Stavisker Fischman.

GRADUATION PHOTOGRAPH
Photograph of Rose Stavisker at her graduation from Columbia University, School of Dental and Oral Surgery.
New York City, 1905. Gift of Bernard D. Fischman in memory of Rose Stavisker Fischman.

DR. STAVISKER'S

DENTAL OFFICE

92 RIVINGTON STREET   NEW YORK

Business card of Dr. Stavisker's dental office in the family apartment on the Lower East Side, New York City, 1908. Gift of Bernard D. Fischman in memory of Rose Stavisker Fischman.

the heart of the Lower East Side. The Orthodox home Rose grew up in influenced her profoundly. Praying three times daily—a religious obligation mandated for men, not women—was a practice she embraced. Her discipline and seriousness of purpose contributed to academic excellence and to the drive that led her to choose to go to dental school.

It must have been deeply disappointing to contemplate the prospect of deferring her dream for another year. As an observant Jew, however, Rose Stavisker accepted Columbia's response.

Then, a remarkable event occurred at Columbia. Before the Sabbath on which the examination was scheduled, a consensus began to emerge among Rose Stavisker's fellow students about the school's insensitivity. Instigated not by her but by her classmates, the class of fifty-five students unanimously declared that they would refuse to take the examination unless it was given on a day other than Saturday. Columbia quietly reversed itself, and the examination was rescheduled. Rose Stavisker passed, graduating proudly in the class of 1905.

She practiced dentistry for several years in the family apartment on Rivington Street, and then she married, and raised three children. When she returned to her profession, she chose to work at a free dental clinic. In addition, Dr. Stavisker aided the growing number of refugees arriving in New York in the late 1930s from Nazi-threatened Europe, by taking them in and providing Sabbath meals and other assistance.

Rose Stavisker Fischman, a Jewish woman of high principle and far ahead of her time, died suddenly in October 1941. Her children, inspired by her life of devotion, would go on to make their own distinguished contributions to American Jewish life.

THE STEINBERGER SUKKAH

Painted by Aryeh Steinberger during the 1920s and 1930s in Budapest, Hungary. Loan by Jehuda, George, Robert, and Paul, sons of Jeno and Piroska Lindenblatt. Loan by Andor Platschek Weiss, grandson of Aryeh Steinberger. In addition, the Museum acknowledges with appreciation Irene White and Magda Tewner, granddaughters of Aryeh Steinberger. Inscribed with prayers recited during Sukkot and text from the Mishnah tracate sukkah (a Rabbinic document, circa 200), it is filled with scenes of Budapest and the countryside, imaginary views of the land of Israel, and biblical and contemporary figures—including the artist's family. Detail here depicts Moses and the Ten Commandments.

Aryeh Steinberger
Sukkah of the Lion

There lived in Budapest, Hungary, in the years between the world wars, a man who was known within the Orthodox Jewish community as a teacher, a cantor, a ritual slaughterer, and a trade union leader. Above all, he was known as a man of great piety. That man was Aryeh Steinberger.

At the age of sixty-five, Reb Aryeh put down the tools of his trade and picked up the tools of his art. What lay ahead was not a placid retirement but the flowering of his greatest creative gifts as a ceremonial scribe and artist.

Reb Aryeh was commissioned to draft ritual documents for members of the community: *ketubot* (marriage contracts), mezuzot (doorpost scrolls), tefillin (phylacteries), *gittin* (bills of divorce). For his family, he created major works, including a fully illustrated Passover Haggadah, a perpetual calendar, a Purim megillah, and a *sefer* Torah for each granddaughter, to be sold as her marriage dowry. Many of these objects survive today, in the family's keeping, on both sides of the Atlantic.

His most ambitious project, however, in both depth and scope, was a sukkah canvas that covered the walls of the Steinberger family sukkah. It is this unique panorama, which he worked on throughout the 1920s and 1930s, that profoundly reflects his love of family, his self-taught artistic technique, and his vision of contemporary as well as spiritual life. It is an exemplary model of the melding of the factual and the fanciful, as Reb Aryeh depicts the details of everyday Hungarian life alongside images of biblical events, the cycle of holidays, and even his idealized view of a city he had never seen—Jerusalem, the beloved home of his heart. With its meticulous calligraphy and ornate tableaux, the sukkah became celebrated within Budapest in its day, and hundreds of people came to view it each year.

With the passage of time, the artist replaced and refined elements of the sukkah

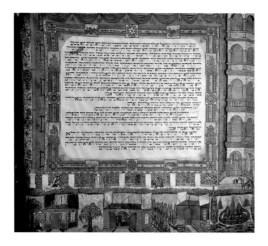

Details from the Steinberger sukkah.

cover. Among the animals included is a magnificent lion, which was his signature: his own name, *Aryeh,* in Hebrew means "lion." Of particular interest is his treatment of the human face. In his earlier scenes the faces are not clearly defined, following the belief that it was a violation of the Third Commandment to make an image of God. But as he was increasingly taken with the desire to paint humans into the narrative, he sought, and received, the permission of the rabbis to do so. The canvas then came to include the traditionally honored guests invited into the sukkah—Abraham, Isaac, Jacob, Joseph, Moses, Aaron, and David—given clear form and detail.

As remarkable as the sukkah cover itself is the saga of its journey, over two continents and half a century, to become the single largest piece of art in the Museum's collection.

Aryeh had two children, Salomon and Regina. A widower, he had made his home with Regina and her family. At the age of eighty-two, Reb Aryeh put down his pen for the last time. As the winds of war swirled about him, he died peacefully, never to know of the terrible fate that awaited over one-half of Hungarian Jews—never to know that his son-in-law would be shot into the Danube; that a grandson would die of typhus at Mauthausen; that a granddaughter, with her two little girls, would be gassed at Auschwitz-Birkenau.

In March 1944, a year and a half after Aryeh's death, the Nazis marched into Hungary—and nothing was safe. Regina's teenage son, Andor, was sent with the sukkah cover to the basement of the vast Dohany Street synagogue, to bury it among other religious treasures.

When the Soviet forces liberated Budapest in January 1945, most of the family, miraculously, had managed to survive the war. Regina's daughter, Piroska, now married to Jeno Lindenblatt and the mother of three small sons, reclaimed the sukkah cover from its hiding place. Piroska was its appropriate guardian because she was not only the eldest of Aryeh's grandchildren still in Hungary, but his spiritual descendant as well: in her were melded his compassion and artistic creativity. As a girl, she had helped him mix his paints, and he had taught her painting, needlepoint, crocheting, and embroidery.

The canvas lay in the back of a closet in her home until October 1956, when the hunger and oppression of Communist rule culminated in the Hungarian Revolution—and for a brief time, the borders were penetrable in a few spots. One by one, Piroska's three oldest children—Jehuda, George, and Robert, now teenagers—escaped into Austria. Last to come were Piroska and Jeno, with ten-year-old Paul (his Hebrew name is Aryeh, after his great-grandfather). Leaving everything else behind, Piroska took the sukkah cover. After the first escape attempt failed, they traveled in the back of a truck, by train, and on foot. By the time the Red Cross rescued them at the Austrian border, Piroska was trudging barefoot in the snow. She had to be carried to their van. Rolled up like a scroll, covered in an old raincoat, the canvas never left her sight. Wrapped in that raincoat was her heritage—the past and the future.

The sukkah cover, accompanied by the Lindenblatts, arrived in the

United States on a plane in April 1957. It had been carried by hand all the way. Its new home was a closet in Piroska and Jeno's apartment, in Williamsburg, Brooklyn, where it was taken out, unrolled, and pieced together for any interested visitor—always with enormous pride by the family.

With Piroska's death in 1983, the rolled canvas passed to a closet in the home of Jehuda, her eldest son. Then, in 1990, a scout from the Museum who was conducting research in the Borough Park section of Brooklyn happened upon a pharmacy and struck up a conversation with the pharmacist. His name was Paul Lindenblatt, Piroska's youngest son. Soon the researcher was sitting in Paul's living room, watching home movies of wartime Budapest. Paul mentioned that he and his brothers had another item that might interest the Museum—a sukkah canvas painted by their great-grandfather.

The results of that conversation are now on display for all to see. Speaking of the family's initial reluctance to share their private possession with the Museum, Robert Lindenblatt says, "It was an extremely difficult decision. But for history, we felt it was our responsibility to show it to the world."

The Steinberger sukkah, like the family for whom it was created, embodies the central theme of the Museum: a rich European prewar culture, the struggle for survival, and, finally, a revitalization. Reb Aryeh's canvas has come a long, long way.

Portrait of artist Aryeh Steinberger. Budapest, Hungary, 1930s. Gift of Lindenblatt Family.

ROSH HASHANAH CARD
Holiday card made by Heinz Motulski. Dresden, Germany, 1930. Gift of Henry Morley. Using colored pencils, eleven-year-old Heinz decorated this Rosh Hashanah card, then added flower cutouts.

Henry Morley
"As if I did not exist"

Heinz Motulski had always excelled at his studies, and the principal of his high school in Dresden had quietly encouraged him. Heinz was grouped in the back row with the high achievers, and the fact that he was the only Jewish boy in his class never had seemed to matter.

Yet, when he entered his classroom on the first day in September 1935, his world was transformed: all the boys, including his best friend, were wearing the uniform of the Hitler Youth, with its prominent swastika armband. The virulently anti-Semitic newspaper, *Der Stuermer,* was pinned up on the walls of the classroom. On the blackboard in front, in immense letters, someone had scrawled "Jew Motulski."

Heinz then noticed that his seat was occupied by another student. None of his fellow students said hello: they treated him as if he were invisible. When the teacher entered, he placed Heinz in an isolated chair in the front row, with the lowest achievers.

From that day forward, the teacher refused to call on him when he raised his hand. In the school yard or walking to and from class, no one would speak to him. In gym class, when the boys boxed, Heinz was regularly paired with a student in a heavier weight class to ensure that he would be beaten up.

For the next three years, he was ignored and demeaned to the point of complete isolation. Heinz knew his parents would take him out of the school if he told them about his treatment. So he kept silent in order to graduate. The price he had to pay, in addition to the daily indignities and cruelties at school, was to live as an emotional stranger within his own family.

In 1936, in the midst of this crisis, Heinz Motulski met Lottie Apt. A student at the nearby girls' high school, she became Heinz's confidante. They met while riding bicycles, and she sensed he had a lot on his mind. Heinz, too, sensed an emotional connection deeper than friendship. The natural urgency of young adults trying to understand their own identity while negotiating the humiliation and pressure of life under the Nazis accelerated the pace of their relationship. Heinz began to think that if they and their families could ever find a way to escape the unfolding Nazi terror, he would ask Lottie to be his wife.

Heinz Motulski's experience of malevolent ostracism in school mirrored what was being unleashed against Jews throughout German society. At the time he had returned to his high school in the fall of 1935, the Nuremberg Laws codified the anti-Semitic principles of Nazi ideology.

As a reaction, Heinz, Lottie, and other young Jews began to live dual lives. Although excluded from all public cultural life, they organized their own house parties and participated in the Jewish community's own newly expanded sports clubs and cultural events in Dresden. Struggling for normalcy, they organized themselves into scouting groups and went hiking, camping, and biking.

More than one hundred thousand Jews emigrated by 1938, but many, including Heinz's and Lottie's families, still waited—and hoped. Heinz's compassionate high school principal awarded Heinz's diploma in private, so that Heinz might be spared humiliation at the official graduation. He confided to him when he handed Heinz his diploma: "The political climate is like a wave. Now there is an upsurge, but it will recede again, and then it will be over."

But the reign of terror had barely begun. On November 9 and 10, 1938, Kristallnacht erupted, the orchestrated national pogrom and assault on the Jews of Germany and Austria. On the first night, at his relatives' apartment, Heinz was told that the Leipzig synagogue had been set on fire and that he must run with them to the nearby park to hide. Some instinct told Heinz not to flee, and indeed, his relatives who went to the park were arrested. The men were sent by the Gestapo to Buchenwald, one of the concentration camps established by the Nazis to detain their political enemies.

Thousands of Jews were detained at Buchenwald and other camps in the roundups following Kristallnacht. Hun-

Identification card for Heinz Motulski. Dresden, Germany, from 1937–1938. Gift of Henry Morley. When Jews in Nazi Germany became impoverished, Jewish social agencies cared for them. Motulski worked as a volunteer for Jewish Winter Relief. This card authorized Motulski to collect clothing for the agency.

dreds died there—some were murdered, others committed suicide, and still others died from heart attacks and other illnesses exacerbated by the brutalities of imprisonment. Those released, including Heinz's and Lottie's fathers, had to prove to the Nazis that they would emigrate within a specified time in order to gain their freedom. They also had to divest themselves of their property and possessions. Of course, now the more urgent challenge became, with so many suddenly wanting to escape, where could they go?

Fortunately, in response to Kristallnacht, England briefly liberalized its immigration policies, permitting entrance to limited numbers of immigrants who promised to work as domestic servants and farmworkers. Lottie Apt and her parents managed to go there, while Heinz's parents traveled to Cuba and then to the United States. Heinz chose to follow Lottie.

In July 1939, two months before war broke out in Europe, Heinz and Lottie were reunited in London. They refused to speak German, as an expression of revulsion at what Germany had become under Hitler, and to accelerate their adjustment to their new country.

Heinz Motulski changed his name to Henry Morley. He enlisted in the British army and worked in a battalion that did the dangerous work of clearing away damaged structures that had been bombed by the Germans in London. In 1946, Henry and Lottie came to the United States to start their family and rebuild their lives.

Henry Morley

Program for a Jewish Cultural Association concert, Berlin, Germany, December 22–23, 1934. Gift of Henry Morley. The Jewish community sponsored its own programs when Jewish performers and artists were no longer allowed to participate in general cultural events.

Membership card for Heinz Motulski, Jewish Cultural Association. Dresden, Germany, 1939. Gift of Henry Morley. This card allowed Motulski to attend events sponsored by the Jewish Cultural Association (Kulturbund).

ORPHANAGE KEYS

Auerbach orphanage keys carried by Selma Plaut. Berlin, Germany, circa 1920s–1930s. Gift of Rabbi W. Gunther and Elizabeth S. Plaut. Jonas Plaut directed the Auerbach orphanage from 1922 to 1939, with the aid of his wife, Selma, who carried the keys in a small leather bag.

Jonas and Selma Plaut

"Whoever rears an orphan, it is as if he has brought him into the world."

– Joshua Ben Karha, Tractate Sanhedrin, Babylonian Talmud

The boys and girls, ages six to sixteen, whom Jonas and Selma Plaut looked after in Berlin in the fall of 1938, were in grave danger. Jonas Plaut, with help from his wife, Selma, was the director of the Baruch Auerbach Institute for the Education of Orphans, and their wards were both orphans and Jews.

After holding positions as a teacher and principal in Jewish secondary schools in Muenster, Germany, Jonas Plaut assumed the directorship of the Auerbach orphanage in Berlin in 1922. Established in 1838, it was a pioneering institution, one of the first modern Jewish orphanages in Europe. The Auerbach's progressive policies were a model not only within the Jewish community, but also throughout the child-welfare world in Germany and abroad.

The Plauts, who lived in a comfortable apartment on the premises, carried out an enlightened policy that was informed by the notion that society's least—its orphans—should have its best: the best teachers and living conditions, as well as an emotionally stable, supportive, and loving environment. There were modern facilities; substantial theater, literary, and cultural activities; and up to 125 residents. There was even a synagogue in the building. To build character and leadership, the boys ran the services on their own. As if they were their parents, the Plauts also sent all the children to Jewish religious schools in the community.

The Plauts had their own children, W. Gunther and Walter. Gunther Plaut was among the last Jewish students to earn a doctorate at the University of Berlin before the banning of Jewish students and the firing of Jewish professors.

In German society, which was increasingly dominated by Nazi racial ideology, the Auerbach's commitment to children was well known and widely respected. The high standards, demanding curriculum, outstanding physical plant, and even an alumni association that in 1936 numbered three hundred members made the orphanage more like a private school than an institution for the poor. It attracted significant financial benefactors in the community and as a result was well funded.

If the Plauts discovered students at the orphanage with intellectual potential, they also provided for academic high school and university education as well as specialized training. Girls also went on to productive lives, and the Plauts even provided a dowry, if necessary. Students from the Baruch Auerbach Institute for the Education of Orphans would grow up to become unusually accomplished people—among them ambassadors, photographers, and renowned musicians.

By the fall of 1938, the terror campaign to force Jews to emigrate had resulted in the departure of tens of thousands of Jews from Germany. Many with means left the country if they were able to find relatives or an employer in a host country to sponsor them. Still, Jonas and Selma Plaut continued to run the orphanage. The Plauts even began to admit nonorphan boys in 1937 and 1938, since Jewish boys who had come to Berlin to go to public school suddenly found themselves, by order of the Nazis, not permitted to attend. Jewish schools were now under a severe strain because of the extra numbers of students.

Formal family portrait of Jonas and Selma Plaut with their son, W. Gunther. Berlin-Charlottenburg, Germany, circa 1913. Gift of Rabbi W. Gunther and Elizabeth S. Plaut.

On the same day as the Kristallnacht pogroms in Germany, Jonas and Selma Plaut's son Gunther, who had gone to study at the Hebrew Union College in Cincinnati in 1935, married Elizabeth Strauss. For the Plauts, the joy of the day was mixed with agonizing family discussions about the sustainability of the orphanage and the fate of its children. Where could they all go?

In February 1939, with many Jewish institutions banned by the Nazis, the orphanage was finally dissolved. This step was not taken, however, until arrangements had been completed for forty boys to go by train to a home run by the French branch of the Jewish relief organization Oeuvre de Secours aux Enfants (OSE) near Paris. Another small group of boys was entrusted to a Quaker organization, which successfully brought them to the United States. Two months later, the Plauts were able to send their household items to their son in Cincinnati. Then, they fled to England.

Of the forty children protected by the OSE, most were sent out of Paris in 1940 to the tiny village of Chabannes in Vichy-controlled France. The children lived in a château near the village and were among hundreds sheltered by the courageous citizens even after the war came to Chabannes and the act of sheltering Jews became a serious crime.

In America, W. Gunther Plaut enlisted as a chaplain in the United States Armed Forces. He served with the American infantry unit that liberated the Dora-Nordhausen Concentration Camp complex in Germany. Jonas and Selma Plaut, who worked with refugee children in England throughout the war, joined their sons in the United States in 1945, Walter having immigrated in 1937. Most of the boys from the Baruch Auerbach Institute for the Education of Orphans who were hidden in Chabannes survived the war. Rabbi W. Gunther Plaut, inspired in part by the experience of his family, devoted himself unceasingly to Jewish and human rights causes. Walter, too, became a rabbi and won great renown as a freedom rider.

Jonas Plaut died in 1948 at the age of sixty-eight. Selma, having received her B.A. at the University of Toronto when she became a centenarian, died at the age of 103.

Photograph of girls eating in the Auerbach orphanage. Berlin, Germany, circa 1925. Gift of Rabbi W. Gunther and Elizabeth S. Plaut.

TORAH SCROLL

From the Bornplatz synagogue, brought to the United States by the Bamberger family in 1940. Hamburg, Germany. Gift of Joseph A. Bamberger and Family. On Kristallnacht, the Gestapo came looking for Seligmann Baer Bamberger; however, he was not at home. He was saving this Torah—a courageous act that saved him from arrest.

Bamberger Family

"I can still hear the loud rap at the front door. . . ."

As Joseph Bamberger remembered it, there was at first a loud stomping of heavy leather boots on the wooden floor in the hallway of the family's apartment building. It was a menacing, echoing sound that grew suddenly nearer. Then there was loud, insistent rapping on their door.

"Who is it?" ten-year-old Joseph's mother asked. "Who's there?"

It was November 9, 1938, at the home of Seligmann and Else Bamberger, and their children, Hannah and Joseph, in Hamburg, Germany. None of them forgot that night, called Kristallnacht (Night of Broken Glass) because of the shards of broken glass from the hundreds of stores, homes, and venerable synagogues that were attacked, looted, destroyed, and burned. It was the first large-scale, organized physical attack on the Jewish community by the Nazi hierarchy all across Germany and Austria.

"Gestapo," came the reply. "Open up."

Two uniformed men barged in and began to search each room, closet, and even the bedclothes. Yet the person they sought was not there. Dr. Seligmann Bamberger, graduate of the University of Wuerzburg, teacher of chemistry and physics at the Jewish Carolienenstrasse school, and devoted leader of his synagogue, had been warned. He was at that moment evading the mobs and making his way through the threatening streets to the Bornplatz synagogue. His mission: To rescue the objects at the very heart of the Jewish community—the Torah scrolls. With the other synagogue leaders, he entered the darkened building and, hoping the scrolls were still there, opened the ark that held them. . . .

For days after Kristallnacht, Dr. Bamberger and the other community leaders hid to avoid arrest. Not all succeeded: more than thirty thousand Jewish and Austrian men throughout Germany were arrested and sent to concentration camps. Anti-Jewish acts had been on the rise, but nothing on this scale had ever occurred.

23

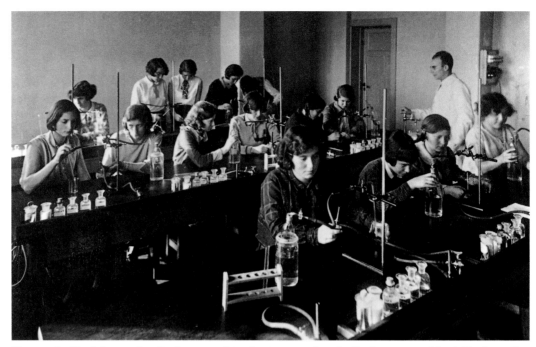

Photograph of Dr. Seligmann Baer Bamberger teaching chemistry to girls at the Carolienenstrasse School. Hamburg, Germany, 1930. Collection of Joseph A. and Dorothy Frank Bamberger.

Personal and community objects of all kinds—household articles, works of art, religious objects—were looted or destroyed.

Bamberger was able to return home a week later. Yet the message was as clear as the crystal: the Nazis had gotten away with their first large-scale anti-Jewish violence.

In the ensuing months, even while new anti-Jewish edicts were promulgated and enforced, Bamberger continued to teach science and to participate in Jewish cultural life. The family was also working strenuously to obtain visas to the United States. However, the restrictive American immigration quotas were already long-filled. To obtain four nonquota visas, Bamberger needed intervention and help in the United States. Fortunately, one of his closest friends, Edgar Frank, had emigrated with his family shortly before Kristallnacht. For a year and a half he persevered, obtaining the endorsement of Congressman Sol Bloom of New York, and even of Albert Einstein, who had immigrated to the United States in 1933. Finally, when Yeshiva College in New York invited Bamberger to join its Department of Chemistry, the family was offered four precious United States visas.

When they sailed from Italy in March 1940 on the SS *Washington,* they knew that with Europe already at war, and almost all doors now closed to Jews, they were among the lucky ones. Nearly all family and friends left behind perished. His former Hamburg students, who had made Bamberger a personalized farewell Hanukkah booklet, were deported to concentration camps.

Joseph remembered: "The most important item in our suitcases was a Torah scroll . . . one of the Torah scrolls that my father had rescued from the Bornplatz synagogue on Kristallnacht."

With this, they reestablished their religious and personal lives, first in Washington Heights, the northern part of Manhattan, where many German Jewish immigrants settled, and then on the Upper West Side of Manhattan. Joseph grew up and married Edgar Frank's youngest daughter, Dorothy, and settled in Patchogue, Long Island, to raise their sons, David and Michael. The Torah scroll was actively in use in their community synagogues.

The Torah has found a new home as part of the permanent Kristallnacht exhibit at the Museum of Jewish Heritage—A Living Memorial to the Holocaust, where it now has a new use. It tells the story of how Seligmann Bamberger risked his life to save the Torah scroll, and how the Torah saved his life.

Portrait of Edgar and Ruth Frank. Collection of Joseph A. and Dorothy Frank Bamberger.

Wedding photograph of Else Buxbaum and Seligmann Baer Bamberger. Wuerzburg, Germany, May 26, 1921. Gift of Joseph A. and Dorothy Frank Bamberger. The Bamberger Family lived in Germany since at least the 1700s.

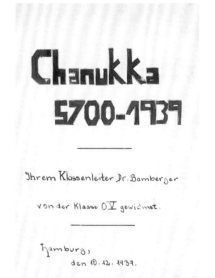

Written by students as a Hanukkah gift for Dr. Seligmann Baer Bamberger, chemistry teacher in a Jewish school. Hamburg, Germany, 1939. Gift of Joseph A. Bamberger and Family. With Hebrew headings from the Haggadah, students recounted anecdotes about their school and themselves. Dr. Bamberger later added handwritten notes about each student, including the date of the student's deportation or death, if known.

SS *ST. LOUIS* PHOTOGRAPH ALBUM

Purchased on board the *St. Louis* by Heinz Grunstein with his six-year-old son, Gerd. Germany, May–June 1939. Lent by the Granston Family (born Grunstein) of London, England. The Grunsteins supplemented official photos with snapshots taken on board. Father and son survived the war as refugees in Britain.

Gerald Granston and Judith Steel

The Voyage of the SS St. Louis

The SS *St. Louis* sailed from Hamburg en route to Cuba on May 13, 1939, with some nine hundred Jewish refugees on board, including six-year-old Gerd Grunstein and fourteen-month-old Judith Koeppel. The passengers did not know that the invasion of Poland and the outbreak of World War II were less than four months away. As the passengers moved about the deck and the *St. Louis* slowly maneuvered out of the harbor, the mood on board was festive. Gerd explored the ship from bow to stern and was already making friends with an attentive German crew and a thoughtful captain.

And why should the passengers not be happy and even giddy with a sense of relief? After all, these refugees had managed to secure passage on a luxury liner—one of the last passenger ships to leave Germany. They were leaving behind the Nazis' increasingly violent anti-Semitic policies, which had led to Kristallnacht. Many were looking forward to starting new lives in America after some time in Cuba. A number of passengers, having been released by luck or bribery from German concentration camps, were now taking in not only the fresh sea air but also their first breaths of freedom in months.

Like most of the passengers, Judith Koeppel's parents, Joseph and Irmgard, had purchased landing permits for Cuba. These were routine documents that would normally require no fee but that, in this instance, had to be purchased from a corrupt Cuban official at exorbitant prices. Many of the refugees were fortunate enough to have U.S. immigration quota numbers, which would eventually entitle them to immigrate to America. All they had to do was cross the Atlantic and set foot in Havana. There, and certainly in the United States, where relatives already awaited some of the passengers, they would finally cease being persecuted because they were Jews.

As the voyage began, Gerd Grunstein was thrilled to skip around on the deck. He bothered his father, Heinz, in their first-class cabin; he watched Captain Gustav Schroeder read the gauges on the *St. Louis*'s bridge—Gerd had the run of the ship. When he grew tired or hungry, he rushed below, where the sailors were happy to share with him their meal of wurst, bread, and beer. There were souvenir photo albums to buy, and like many of the passengers, Gerd's father (his mother had died in 1938) took his own photographs as well, so that they could remember their voyage to freedom.

This all changed dramatically when, fourteen days later, the ship entered Cuban territorial waters. To the consternation of the passengers, Cuban officials refused to come aboard to begin the immigration process. As the hours dragged on, Joseph and Irmgard Koeppel, holding Judy in their arms, gathered into a worried knot of passengers looking down over the railing as only twenty-two people were allowed off the ship—only those, it turned out, whose landing permits were issued before May 6. To the passengers' total shock, it was announced that all the other permits purchased after the sixth would not be honored, including those of Gerd's and Judy's parents.

Family members of some of the passengers, who had come out into the harbor on small boats to locate their relatives, were not allowed on board. They could only shout up to their loved ones straining helplessly over the *St. Louis*'s railing. Something had to be done. Morris Troper and Lawrence Berenson, representatives of the American Jewish Joint Distribution Committee, tried to negotiate the disembarkation of the refugees. They failed. The ship would have to leave.

While new appeals were being launched through diplomatic channels, the *St. Louis* left Havana on June 2. Hoping to buy time and catch the world's attention, a sympathetic Captain Schroeder steered the *St. Louis* toward the Straits of Florida, near American territorial waters. Reporters in the United States wrote spirited stories, newsreels were made of the refugees' plight, and still they waited. With the lights of Miami and other coastal cities visible in the distance, Gerd's and Judy's parents were at least able to renew their optimism.

Finally, American immigration officials announced, on June 5, that the refugees would not be allowed to enter the United States. With this last hope

Photograph of Gerd Grunstein on board the SS *St. Louis,* 1939. Lent by the Granston Family (born Grunstein) of London, England.

crushed, Gerd remembered his father turning to him with a worried face, asking, "If I jump into the water, would you hold on to me and lie on my back while I swim to the shore?"

All options exhausted for the moment, the *St. Louis* turned and began its traumatic return voyage to the Nazi nightmare. There was minimal food and water on the boat, but most of all there was a growing hopelessness and barely controlled frenzy because the passengers saw their return to Germany as a death sentence. Where could they go? Stateless and with only the possessions they carried, where could they turn? By the time the *St. Louis* docked at Antwerp, four countries—England, France, Belgium, and Holland—had announced they would each accept approximately a fourth of the *St. Louis*'s passengers.

Gerd and Heinz Grunstein transferred to the *Rhakotis,* a German ship bound for England. Unlike the crew of the St. Louis, the *Rhakotis* sailors taunted the six-year-old boy with a chant that stayed with him all his life: "Don't think you are getting away. Jew pigs, we will get you in the end."

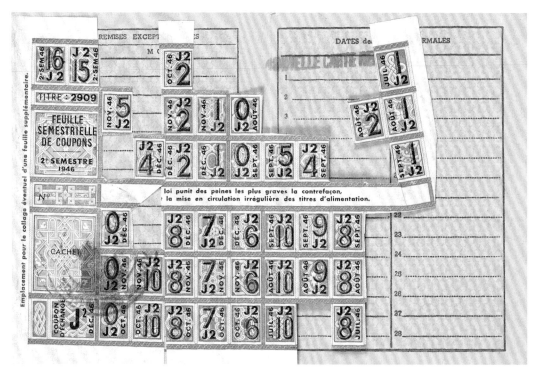

French identity card and ration book for Judith Koeppel. France, 1946–1947. Gift of Judith Steel, Yaffa Eliach Collection, donated by the Center for Holocaust Studies.

With the Nazi occupation of France, Belgium, and Holland, many of the *St. Louis*'s passengers would eventually be caught up again in the Nazis' web; yet most would somehow find a way to survive. Along with those who went to England, Gerd and his father also survived. When the *Rhakotis* landed in Southampton, the little boy was so deliriously happy that he spent the entire day saying "Good morning," the only words in English he knew, to everyone in sight. The Grunsteins spent the war years in London in relative safety.

Not so for Judith Koeppel and her parents. After disembarking from the *St. Louis* in Belgium, Judy and her parents were sent to France. After France was invaded and occupied in June 1940, they hid for more than two years. Eventually they were discovered and arrested. Judith was old enough to remember the frantic cries of her frail grandfather as he was taken by French police to Gurs, a camp in the south of France that was a transit point for shipment to death camps in Poland.

Sensing they were now trapped, Joseph and Irmgard Koeppel made the agonizing decision to entrust their daughter to the Oeuvre de Secours aux Enfants (OSE), a French branch of a Jewish relief organization that was able to hide their child with a Catholic family. In the embrace of this family, the Enards, who took her regularly to church for her protection but never tried to convert her, Judith Koeppel survived the war. She learned later that her parents had been deported to Auschwitz-Birkenau, where they were murdered.

When Judith arrived in New York in 1946 to live with her uncle and aunt, the ship she was on, the *Athos II,* was carrying sixty-eight other orphaned children of the Holocaust. At the time, an East Coast maritime strike prevented all ships from docking. The federal government, however, interceded on behalf of the orphans, and the ship was able to dock and to deliver the children to their waiting relatives.

Gerald Granston and Judith Steel

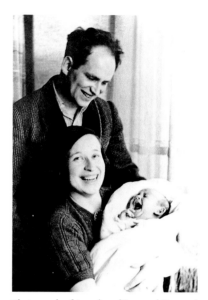

Photograph of Joseph and Irmgard Koeppel with their daughter, Judith. Berlin, Germany, 1938. Gift of Judith Steel, Yaffa Eliach Collection, donated by the Center for Holocaust Studies.

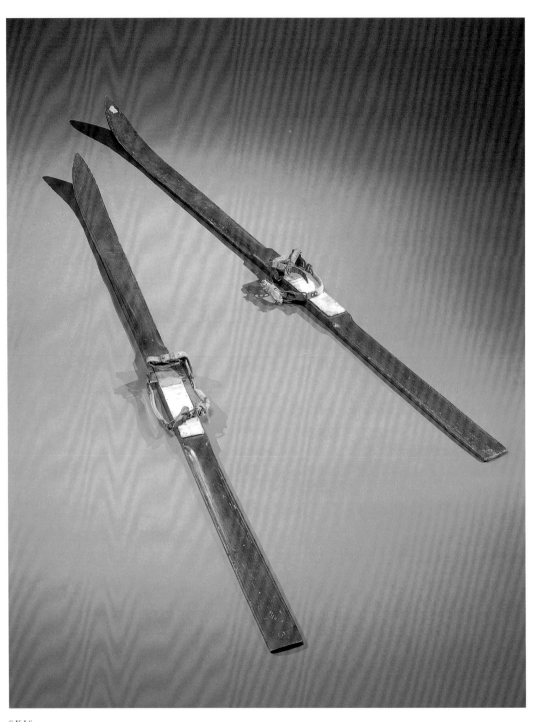

SKIS

Used by Helene Ehrlich to escape to Sweden. Norway, spring 1941. Gift of Robert, Kornelia, Thomas, and Kate Ehrlich. In Norway, Ehrlich gathered information for the resistance while working as a cleaning woman for the Germans. When she was discovered, she fled to Sweden on these skis.

Helene Ehrlich
Skiing to Freedom

In flight from the Nazis since Hitler's rise to power in 1933, Helene Ehrlich was used to moving fast, but rarely, if ever, on skis. Now, at age forty-two, she was struggling to keep up with her much younger traveling partner as they zigzagged through the snow-filled forest on the Norway-Sweden border.

This was no vacation. The snow in places was often too deep and thick for skiing, and the temperature nearly thirty degrees below zero. It was April 1941, a year after the Nazis had invaded Norway. Ehrlich, a German Jewish refugee working for the Norwegian resistance in Oslo, was fleeing the Gestapo and skiing for her life.

When she sat down to rest, one of her skis began slipping down the hill. Although she lunged for it, the ski was gone, and Ehrlich was now certain her long, tortuous odyssey as a stateless Jewish refugee would come to an end in a Nazi jail cell, or on the gallows.

As her partner skied on to the top of the mountain without her, Ehrlich sat exhausted and bewildered in the snow. She had every reason to think she would never see her children again.

She remembered them now, crying and holding hands, not wanting to part from her, on that morning in Prague two and a half years earlier, on November 27, 1938. Having arrived in Prague from Nuremberg in 1933 without documents or money, Ehrlich had labored at the most menial jobs in order to support the twins and to obtain transportation and visas. Finally, in the last frantic days before Hitler moved into Czechoslovakia, visas had arrived from the United States—but only for the children.

At the last possible moment, through the intervention of the local Jewish community and the Norwegian humanitarian organization Nansenhjelpen, she became one of twenty-six people to whom the Norwegian consulate issued a

"Nansen" passport for stateless people. With only one suitcase and a picture of her children, Helene Ehrlich arrived in Oslo.

There, those who had been persecuted were housed, fed, and even feted by Norwegian officials. Ehrlich cleaned the ceilings and walls of the king of Norway's palace, and her gratitude was boundless. Full of hope, she went to the United States consulate, determined to secure permission to go to America to join her children; she was turned down. She then tried to stow away on a Norwegian ship bound for America but was discovered.

Then, on April 9, 1940, barely more than a year since she had escaped them in Czechoslovakia, the Nazis violated Norway's announced neutrality and occupied the country. As German tanks pushed through the streets of Oslo, Ehrlich made a fateful decision: she had had enough of fleeing. She would honor and repay the Norwegians by joining their underground.

Within days of the occupation, she found a job as a cleaning woman in a building housing German military personnel. As she moved from office to office—with her pail and broom, to all the world a simple cleaning lady—she memorized documents left on desktops. By now she was fluent in Norwegian, and the Nazis did not suspect that German was her native language. She committed to memory fragments of the officers' conversations. Regularly, she reported the information to her contacts in the Norwegian resistance.

The dangerous work went well for a year, but then the Germans, who were now secretly planning the invasion of Russia for June 1941, tightened their security. Ehrlich suspected she was about to be discovered, which would mean torture and death.

By another inexplicable stroke of luck, a German officer approached her as they were riding the elevator alone. "You must disappear," he said. "The Gestapo knows who you are."

She reported this to her underground group leader and then went into hiding. Many Norwegians, struggling to get to England through Sweden to join the government-in-exile there, had already frozen to death on the border. Increasingly, Norwegian Jews and Jewish refugees such as Ehrlich were being arrested and deported. The resistance would have to find an inventive way to get her across the border. They recruited a guide and another woman: the ruse would be three girls having a lovely time on a skiing vacation.

Photograph of Helene Ehrlich. Stockholm, Sweden, 1944. Gift of Robert, Kornelia, Thomas, and Kate Ehrlich. Helene sent this photo to her children in the United States, from whom she had been separated since 1938.

Only now the "vacation" had turned into a nightmare, and Ehrlich was lost, without her ski, somewhere in the forbidden three-mile zone separating the two borders. Suddenly, her partner reappeared and was heading down the hill toward her—not to retrieve her but to shout in panic, "Run, the Germans are coming!"

Within seconds, two soldiers were pointing their rifles at Ehrlich's head, and she fainted. When she revived, she found her captors to be not Germans, but *landfiskales,* Swedish officials collaborating with the Germans and the puppet government of Norway. While her traveling partner, a Norwegian citizen, was allowed to cross the border and to take the train to Stockholm, Ehrlich—stateless, Jewish, and a refugee—was detained and interrogated. Refusing to reveal anything about her underground contacts or the route they had taken, she was thrown in jail. Exhausted, she was sent by the *landfiskales* back into the forest on the Swedish side of the border where she had been apprehended—there to face, as many others had before her, a painful death from exposure.

After some hours, the jail's warden and his wife—who opposed the collaborationists—rescued Ehrlich. They brought her to their home and nursed her slowly back to health. They became her advocates, appealing to the *landfiskales* to permit her to remain in Sweden. Intervention, ultimately through King Gustaf of Sweden, led her to freedom from custody and to a train ticket to Stockholm.

Once again in a strange country, with another language she did not speak, she sustained herself with the hope of reuniting with her children. Yet the danger had by no means passed. Unlike Norway, Sweden, though technically neutral, tipped toward Germany and allowed German troop trains to pass through its territory. Ehrlich joined with protesting Swedish humanitarian organizations, but she had to watch herself even though the war was nearing its end.

The war was over for more than a year before Ehrlich was able to secure a visa and transportation to the United States—on a coal freighter. It had been eight years since she had seen her children. When her twins—no longer small children— greeted her at the dock, she had with her the old wooden skis. The Swedish police had retrieved the one that was lost, so that she could ski out of the woods in their custody. The skis were by now very worn, the leather straps were frayed, and the hemp bindings threadbare, but they were the skis that had carried her to freedom.

PHOTOGRAPH OF SIMON KORT AND HIS STUDENTS

Civitella Internment Camp, Italy. Gift of Joan E. Gerstler in memory of Simon Kort. Kort is seen standing in the background holding a book, with his students seated around a table in their makeshift classroom. The inscription on the back of the photo reads in Italian, "To the kind Mr. Kort. From Bina and Ida."

Simon Kort

"We are students of Signor Kort"

"A man tall sixteen feet showed him the house of my uncle," reads the intriguing translation error of an Italian sentence in the notebooks of Ida Labi, a young Jewish refugee from Tripoli, Libya. She has charmingly mistranslated "sixteen" for "six."

Ida had an unusual instructor, Simon Kort, a Berlin-born former employee of an Italian electrical company in Milan. He was working hard and resourcefully to teach Ida and his other students English. The year was 1941, the school was improvised inside a hospital, and while there were no armed guards in the classroom—Simon Kort's married friends could even be visited by their wives—neither teacher nor pupils had freedom. For they were all prisoners of the Italian Fascist government of Benito Mussolini. They were being interned in a small town, Civitella del Tronto, in south central Italy.

Having come to Italy via Germany from Czechoslovakia with his father in 1935 seeking economic opportunity, Kort, at age twenty-five, decided to stay on in Milan when his father returned to Czechoslovakia. Compared to the increasingly violent anti-Semitism practiced by the Nazis in Germany and in the countries they had already invaded in the late 1930s, life in Italy was tolerable for *Emigranten,* political refugees, such as Simon. As late as 1936, Mussolini was still engaged in a balancing act, on the one hand currying Hitler's favor and on the other hand meeting with Zionist leaders, calling for the establishment of a Jewish state, and tolerating Jewish refugees.

All this changed, however, with the German-Italian intervention in the Spanish Civil War as allies of Franco. In 1938, Italy promulgated Nuremberg-style racial laws. However, they were applied with a pronounced lack of enthusiasm: Italy and Italian-occupied territories, such as Libya, became havens for persecuted Jews.

Notebook used by Ida Labi, with lessons in English and Italian. Civitella Internment Camp, Italy, 1944. Gift of Joan E. Gerstler in memory of Simon Kort.

37

Simon Kort was among the thousands of Jews with foreign nationality in Italy who, lacking any official status, were ordered to leave in 1938. For those, like Kort, who evaded the expulsion order, there were *razzias,* or roundups, and many foreign Jews were arrested and deported. For two years, the police issued individual *fogli di via,* orders to leave Italy at once, but where was Simon Kort to go? With his resourcefulness, linguistic abilities, and network of friends, he managed for months to continue to avoid arrest. When Italy entered the war in June 1940, the situation deteriorated badly. There were mass arrests, apartments were raided frequently, and there were early morning roundups.

Kort was apprehended with others in August 1940. A month later, humiliatingly manacled in pairs, the arrested were driven in police vans to the Milan railroad station. From there they were transported to an internment camp in Tossicia, an isolated mountain village in the province of Teramo. In January 1941, Kort was transferred to Civitella del Tronto, also in Teramo, where he was interned in an abandoned hospital. Kort and other German and Polish Jews—business people, mechanics, artists, musicians, and even an Orthodox rabbi who had run a kosher restaurant in Venice—received matzoh from Italian Jews and managed to celebrate Passover that year.

At the end of 1941, Kort and the European Jews were fascinated to see the arrival of a group of Sephardic Jews from Libya. There were sixty of them—men, women, and children in families. Under pressure from the Nazis, harsh anti-Jewish measures were being instituted against them. They had been transported from Tripoli, an Italian colony in North Africa, and other places in Libya.

The German and Polish Jews affectionately called them their "Tripolini." The Libyan Jews spoke Arabic, although some spoke Italian, and everyone was dressed—to the Europeans' eyes—in exotic Arab clothing. Originally from Malta and Gibraltar, and considered British subjects, they had been accused by the Italians of collaborating with the Allies during the summer of 1940, when the British army had successfully advanced against the Italians. When German general Rommel drove the British out in early 1941, the returning Italians deported these Jewish families to Civitella del Tronto in central Italy, and into the classroom of Simon Kort.

The Libyans struggled to keep kosher and to advance their children's education, which is where Simon Kort came in. He improvised a school in the hospital and taught the Libyan children English. There were other subjects as well, including Italian, mathematics, and Hebrew. Although life was difficult and dangerous, concentration camp conditions did not prevail here for either the Libyan or the European Jews. Red Cross packages arrived, and new internees, if they had money, were even being permitted to live in the village itself.

All this changed dramatically with the Allied invasions, first of Sicily and then of the mainland of Italy at Anzio, north of Naples. The Fascist regime surrendered to the Allies in September 1943, and the country divided in two: the south in the hands of the Allies and in the north a satellite state set up and controlled by the Germans. While Mussolini had been in charge, Italian Fascists had, for their own political reasons, thwarted Nazi pressure for mass deportations of Italian Jews and foreign Jewish nationals. However, as German soldiers moved, for the first time, into Civitella del Tronto, Simon Kort and about twenty of the internees escaped into the countryside.

German regular army units eventually rounded up Kort and the other foreign Jewish men, including the male Libyan Jews, and trucked them south to Pescara. There they were forced to labor at a brickyard to prepare antitank defenses against the approaching British and American forces. Kort and the European Jews translated for the Libyans as various groups of prisoners traded food rations. The situation deteriorated further in April 1944, when the German military police arrived to arrest all Jews who had entered Italy as German nationals. Kort knew time had run out if he was to escape deportation. Saying good-bye to his "Tripolini," he climbed up to the mountains above Civitella del Tronto. There he worked with the partisans as an interpreter and led escaped British prisoners through the German lines between Teramo and Ascoli.

After the war, many of the Libyan Jews, who were protected because they were British subjects, survived and returned home. There they were aided by Jewish soldiers in the Jewish brigade of the British army. However, in the wake of pogroms and riots that broke out after World War II, most Libyan Jews, including those Simon Kort had taught, immigrated to Italy or Israel. In 1947, Simon Kort immigrated to the United States.

Covers of notebooks belonging to Simon Kort's students. Civitella Internment Camp, Italy. Gift of Joan E. Gerstler in memory of Simon Kort.

RADIOGRAM

Send the following Radiogram *"Via RCA"* subject to terms on back hereof, which are hereby agreed to

May 29th, 1941.

Nlt American Consul General   (R. P. $6.-)
Yokohama, Japan

KINDLY REPLY IF VISAS ROJTENBERG BARANOWICZ BRYSKMAN GRANTED OR

IF ANY ADDITIONAL DOCUMENTS REQUIRED STOP I TAKE FULL FINANCIAL

RESPONSIBILITY FOR THEIR LIVING REQUIREMENTS CERTAIN THEY WILL

BECOME LOYAL AMERICAN CITIZENS AND AN ASSET TO OUR COUNTRY

THEREFORE WOULD GREATLY APPRECIATE YOUR KIND ATTENTION. *please grant their visas now.*

JACOB KESTENBAUM

Main Office: 66 Broad Street, New York, N. Y. (Always Open)   Phone: HAnover 2-1811

FULL-RATE MESSAGE UNLESS MARKED OTHERWISE
Sender's Name and Address
(Not to be transmitted)   Kestenbaum Bros. 243 W. 30 St. NYC   Form 100-25-TA-930S

TELEGRAM

Sent by Jacob Kestenbaum in New York to the American Consul General. Yokohama, Japan, circa 1941. Gift of Shirley Schulder. Businessman Jacob Kestenbaum was approached by Rabbi Kalmanowitz to assist Mirrer Yeshiva students stranded in Europe. Kestenbaum employed at least one secretary solely to move paperwork through the State Department to secure affidavits for refugees.

The Mirrer Yeshiva

The Journey of the Mirrer Yeshiva

Founded in 1815 in the small Polish town of Mir, just twenty miles from the Russian border, the Mirrer Yeshiva, one of the most renowned centers of Jewish higher learning in Europe, had risen to many challenges in its history—organizational, academic, and theological. But nothing had quite prepared its three hundred students and faculty members for the odyssey it was about to undertake—a desperate fifteen-thousand-mile flight during World War II across Russian Siberia, Japan, and China.

In April 1939, Moses Zupnik was a twenty-three-year-old German-born student preparing to resume his studies, which he had begun three years before, at the Mirrer Yeshiva. His studies had been interrupted by travel and work as a salesman, but now he was eager to resume the young scholar's life with some of the towering figures of the Talmudic tradition.

However, the yeshiva, or seminary, at Mir was particularly vulnerable to the winds of war beginning to sweep through Europe. When the Nazis invaded Poland in September 1939, the yeshiva's staff and students as a body relocated to Vilna, in neighboring Lithuania, and from there to Kedainiai, twenty-seven miles from Kovno.

Here Zupnik and the other young scholars resumed their studies. The interlude, however, was to be short-lived, as the Soviets occupied all of Lithuania. The yeshiva community was confronting, on the one hand, the Nazis who wanted to kill them and, on the other hand, the Soviets who would likely not let them study Torah or worship God. One wise student, Leib Malin, convincingly urged faculty and students that the hour had come to leave Europe altogether. The Mirrer Yeshiva determined to leave as a group.

Moses Zupnik and several other students traveled from Kedainiai to Kovno, which was then the provisional capital of Lithuania, to obtain the required documents for the entire student and faculty body. The paperwork problem was immense: each of the students needed a visa to exit Lithuania, a transit visa, and, finally, an entry visa to a country that would take them in. Affidavits for entry visas to the United States, funds for transportation, and support along the way also had to be in hand.

Few of the students had any of these documents, and securing them was rendered even more complicated and desperate because, except for a few students such as Zupnik, who had a Polish passport, nearly all of the students were without passports or other identifying papers.

In the summer of 1940, very few consulates remained operating in Lithuania, but there were skeleton staffs in the consulates of Great Britain, Japan, and Holland. A representative of the students, Jacob Eiderman, prevailed on the British consul in charge of Polish affairs to produce more than three hundred temporary documents in lieu of a passport. Extraordinarily, the official produced these documents, each carrying no expiration date, without ever having seen the individual students.

Now the challenge became to find a country to issue documents accepting more than three hundred people at the end of the journey. Another fortuitous connection was made. The Dutch consul in Kovno, Jan Zwartendijk, was persuaded to stamp the passports with the phrase "Valid only for Curaçao," thus arranging for entry for the students to the Dutch-controlled island of Curaçao, in the Caribbean.

The final paperwork challenge became how to obtain transit visas from Japan, for the yeshiva's students and teachers would have to travel through Japan—and likely remain there for some time—before going on to Curaçao.

In late summer 1940, time was especially critical because the Soviets had announced that in three weeks they would remove all the remaining consular officials from Lithuania. However, they indicated to the Mirrer community that if transit visas could be obtained from Japan, they would honor the documents and allow the Yeshiva to travel east through Soviet territory. It was a large "if" indeed.

Taking all the documents with him, Moses Zupnik borrowed a suit from one of his rabbis and stood on line to appeal to the Japanese consul, Chiune Sugihara.

Transit visa issued to Feiga Market, in lieu of a passport, in Lithuanian with Japanese, Russian, English, and French. Kaunas (Kovno), Lithuania, 1940. Gift of Allen Magid. This document carries a permit issued by Chiune Sugihara to pass through Japan en route to the United States.

Because of large crowds attempting to see Sugihara, Zupnik was unable to make his appeal.

Undeterred, he returned the following day with a friend, bribed a guard, and was brought into the consul's offices. When he told Sugihara's assistant that he was requesting more than three hundred transit visas, the man declared that it was impossible. Zupnik prevailed on him for a face-to-face meeting with Sugihara. At first, Sugihara questioned the plan. Then he asked for assurances that there were funds for transportation and accommodations for the long trip and the sojourn in Japan. Zupnik did his best to reassure him.

To plan and finance the institution's escape, eminent scholar Rabbi Abraham Kalmanowitz flew via Sweden to England and then to New York. There he began to work around—and against—the clock to raise large sums of money for transportation for his hundreds of students and teachers. In New York, Rabbi Kalmanowitz successfully appealed to such sympathetic American Jews as businessman Jacob Kestenbaum, who, on an individual basis, had already been sending affidavits of support and funds for transportation to the Mirrer Yeshiva students.

Although his government advised him to reject the Mirrer Yeshiva's request, Sugihara made a personal decision to grant the transit visas. "I cannot allow these people to die," he said later. "Whatever punishment may be imposed upon me, I know I should follow my conscience."

Although Sugihara had only just met Moses Zupnik, he accepted the student's offer to assist the consular office with the issuing of visas. For the next several weeks, Zupnik worked day and night to help Sugihara's staff to prepare and to stamp visas, not only for the Mirrer Yeshiva students but also for many other refugees. Moses Zupnik and the Mirrer Yeshiva "boys" cabled Rabbi Kalmanowitz for the travel money, and the rabbi was able to send forty thousand dollars to Kovno. In groups of forty to fifty, the students and their teachers made their way through Minsk and Moscow, and through Siberia to Vladivostok. Fifteen of their number were arrested by Russian police in Vladivostok; more money was made available for use as bribes, and the arrested were freed. They made their way with the rest of the Mirrer Yeshiva by ship to Kobe, Japan. Moses Zupnik arrived there on the first day of Hanukkah, 1940.

In Kobe, the local Sephardic community, Jews originally from Baghdad, made one of their synagogues available to the Yeshiva students, and here they were finally able to reconstitute their school and resume their studies. But the journey was by no means over.

The odyssey now took a new turn when the Japanese forced the entire Mirrer community to relocate to Shanghai. During the remaining years of the war in that Japanese-occupied city, conditions were harsh but tolerable. A leader of the local Sephardic community offered them the use of a synagogue. Rabbi Kalmanowitz was able to send funds so no member of the community starved. Moses Zupnik and the other Mirrer students set about the business of a yeshiva: they studied. Since they had brought with them on their long journey only individual tractates of the Talmud, and full sets were needed for study, they arranged for entire sets of the Talmud to be printed, as well as other necessary books. Thousands of Jewish books were thus printed in Shanghai.

When the war ended, nearly all of the yeshiva students relocated to the

United States, while one group left for Israel. Thousands of miles from the town of Mir, the yeshivas were formally reconstituted in two new homes—in Brooklyn, New York, and in Jerusalem.

In 1984, Israel's Yad Vashem Holocaust Memorial in Jerusalem awarded Chiune Sugihara the title "Righteous Among the Nations" for his courageous assistance to the Mirrer Yeshiva and other Jewish refugees during World War II.

The Mirrer Yeshiva

DRAWING

From the POW diary of Vladimir Knezic. Germany, October 2, 1944. Gift of Edna Klinovsky and Batya Nachum. While in captivity, Knezic kept a diary in the form of drawings and cartoons. His work was a reflection of his harsh environment and the camaraderie of his fellow inmates. Included in this illustration is a parachutist who is a cook, electrician, and medic.

Vladimir Knezic

The Monthly News from Kommando 2365

In May of 1944, he drew an impishly happy whale breaching the surface of his graph paper, with a Star of David on its nose. A few months later, as the High Holidays approached, his imagery became more traditionally Jewish. He lettered the customary New Year's greeting, *L'shanah tovah tikatevu,* on the masthead of his graph paper. Near it and to the left, covering his drawing of a shovel, he wrote in Yiddish, *Gut Yomtov,* and, to the right, over a drawn block of fifty kilos of cement, he wrote the same New Year's greeting in Serbo-Croatian. He also included a menu for a delicious fantasy holiday feast, with a final course of Camel cigarettes.

The artist was certainly no commander. He was a soldier, a Jew, and a captive of the Nazis; he was, in fact, Sergeant Major Third Class Vladimir Knezic, of the Yugoslav army, prisoner number 11212. These drawings, part of a sardonic graphic record of four years of captivity, also convey wistful good humor and a sense of Jewish identity.

Vladimir Knezic was born Vladimir Kaufman in 1909 in Zagreb, in the province of Croatia. His parents chose to change the family name to Knezic to appear more Yugoslavian in a part of the world where anti-Semitism was no stranger. Nevertheless, as a young child, he studied in a traditional Jewish school, a heder, and Knezic and his sister grew up in a Jewish community with strong Zionist political leanings. At age twenty, he began a career in the Yugoslav army, and during the 1930s rose through the ranks. He married Berta and had a son, Micro.

During the political turmoil that preceded the outbreak of World War II, the Croats, the second-largest group in Yugoslavia, next to the Serbs, were agitating for their own state. In 1930, a violent, ultranationalistic organization, the Ustaše, was formed.

When the Axis powers invaded Yugoslavia in April 1941, a satellite Croatian

Drawing from the POW diary of Vladimir Knezic. Germany, September 17, 1944. Gift of Edna Klinovsky and Batya Nachum. As the High Holidays approached, Knezic drew a holiday edition. On this page, a horn announces the "latest events in words and pictures." Above the horn is the menu for his fantasy holiday feast.

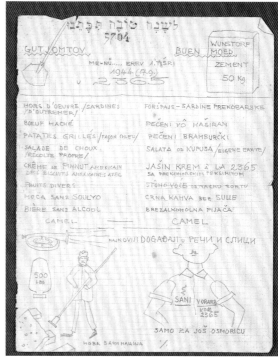

state was set up, with the Nazi-leaning Ustaše governing as puppets. By the summer of 1941, the Ustaše campaign to eliminate the Serbs and Jews had become genocidal. The Yugoslav army resisted the Germans and the Ustaše, but many units were captured, including Vladimir Knezic's.

Mainly on foot and at times by train, the captured soldiers were sent through Macedonia, Bulgaria, and Hungary into Germany. They arrived in midsummer at a camp near Nuremberg. Conditions were extremely harsh. Yet for Jews in Zagreb, where Knezic's family remained and about whom he knew nothing, conditions were far worse. His wife and son were likely caught up in the Ustaše's mass arrest of Jews on June 26, 1941.

Deep inside Germany, in 1942, Vladimir Knezic could not yet know this, although he feared such an outcome. He was now part of a group of four hundred isolated Jewish prisoners of war. Serving the German war machine in Osnabrueck and other locations, they did the backbreaking and dangerous work of slave laborers—but because they were prisoners of war, the Nazis kept them alive in case they could find a way to use the POWs or exchange them.

During these years, Knezic's drawings and cartoons became documentary and

48

satirical, a record of his and his comrades' lives in captivity. It was a kind of monthly news report crafted by Knezic and his friends, seen only by those they trusted. Knezic's graphic record indicates that the POWs worked moving cement blocks and loading artillery shells onto trains. Slowly, as Allied victories mounted, conditions for the POWs, even the Jewish POWs, improved. Knezic's news of May 1944 shows Red Cross packages from Britain, France, America, and Egypt. Radios and newspapers were allowed in September 1944. He recorded in a cartoon in March 1945 the arrival of a group of tattered soldiers, or perhaps slave laborers—Jews, in any event, recognizable by the star on their caps. They were put to work in the mine shaft of a German corporation.

Knezic was now calling himself, on the masthead of his monthly news, Kommando 2365, and would soon proclaim, in one of the final issues, "Liberte." For in fact Vladimir Knezic was liberated in Nuremberg in April 1945. When he was released, he learned that his wife and son had been murdered in Treblinka.

Hounded by the Ustaše when he tried to return to Zagreb, Knezic went to Belgrade and worked in a Jewish orphanage; there he met a Holocaust survivor who became his wife. In 1948, they immigrated to Israel, where they raised two daughters, and that, Kommando 2365 might have agreed, was the best news of all.

Vladimir Knezic

Photograph of Vladimir Knezic taken in 1945 after liberation. Gift of Edna Klinovsky and Batya Nachum.

SHOCHET KNIFE

Given to Rabbi Leon J. Pessah, a ritual slaughterer *(shochet),* by his grandfather, Chacham Yehoshua Matalon. Greece, made circa 1850. Collection of Joseph L. Pessah. Rabbi Pessah slaughtered animals according to Jewish law to provide kosher food for guerrilla forces in the Greek mountains.

Rabbi Leon Pessah
The Fighting Rabbi

He was only five-foot-one; he wore owlish glasses; he was, in appearance and manner, shy and unpretentious. He was a quiet-voiced speaker of numerous languages, a man who might be anything but a partisan warrior.

Yet, Leon (Yehudah) Pessah was a trusted friend of and courier for the anti-Nazi partisan groups in the mountains of Greece during World War II. He was a man so devoted to his books, family, and faith that he three times risked his life to return, alone, to his German-occupied town to retrieve family and ritual objects. Leon Pessah was very much a fighting rabbi and a rabbi fighting for his faith.

Having grown up in Salonika, the large port city on the Greek coast that had been a great religious and cultural center of Sephardic life, Rabbi Pessah had the unwelcome distinction—due to the outbreak of World War II—of being a member of the last graduating class of Salonika's rabbinical seminary. In 1941, after serving in the Greek army, he took his first pulpit in Trikala, a town in the mountains of western Thessaly, where a community of nearly five hundred Jews had lived for centuries. Rabbi Pessah and his wife, Gracia, who was an excellent seamstress, lived in the town, near the schoolhouse, where the rabbi also taught French to the town's children. Among his language students were the children of the local chief of police and the prelate of the Greek Orthodox church. Their admiration and respect for Rabbi Pessah would, eventually, save his life and that of his family.

After invading Greece in April 1941, the Nazis came to Trikala in 1942 to begin their roundups, decimations, and attempt at ultimate destruction of the Jewish community.

Although Rabbi Pessah, his wife, and their infant son, Joseph, were able to evade the roundup, the message was clear: they had to flee in order to survive. The family was able to arrange safe passage to the nearby mountains. The mountain peo-

Photograph of Rabbi Leon J. Pessah with his class. Trikala, Greece, 1945. Collection of Joseph L. Pessah. After the war, Rabbi Pessah returned to the religious school where he had taught before the war. Many of the children had died. Here, Rabbi Pessah poses with students who survived. His son, Joseph Pessah, is at the lower right.

ple, many of whom hated the Nazis, had organized into partisan units and attacked the Nazis in the narrow passes, where the Germans could not bring their vehicles or tanks. Fearing ambush, the Nazis were reluctant to invade the mountains, but when they came close, the partisans moved Jewish families—including the Pessahs—to safer locations.

Rabbi Pessah ventured back to Trikala to retrieve his leather-bound *shochet*'s knife, the ritual slaughterer's implement, in order to help the Jewish guerrilla fighters and their families in the mountains to keep kosher. He also retrieved many of his religious books and astronomical resources, which helped him, when he returned to the mountains, to determine when Passover and the other holidays fell so that they might be observed.

Because he could speak Italian, Greek, French, and other languages and dialects of the area, Rabbi Pessah traveled between the mountains and the towns to relay messages among the various groups of partisans. He was stopped and picked up several times on these dangerous missions. Once, he was even caught with a suitcase of Jewish books. He said he was a simple farmer delivering bags, whose contents he did not know. Once, he was forced to hide for three days with a Greek family. In such encounters, Rabbi Pessah relied on his courage, linguistic skills, ingenuity, and faith to survive. The residents remaining in Trikala also knew that if they turned in the rabbi or collaborated with the Nazis, the partisans would exact punishment.

As Allied units infiltrated Greece to join the partisans, the momentum of the war began to shift. Finally, the Germans evacuated Greece in September 1944. But such moments of optimism and joy could not reverse what had happened in the towns and cities of Greece. Although the Jews living in the small towns of Thessaly, such as Trikala and Volos, were able to survive by hiding in the mountains or dispersing among their courageous neighbors, of the 56,000 Jews living in Salonika in 1941, less than 4 percent survived. Among the killed was the extended family of Rabbi Pessah and his wife.

Although the Trikala synagogue, along with its Torahs and ornaments, had survived—the Greek neighbors had camouflaged it as a warehouse so the Nazis would not destroy it—the Pessah family determined that they should eventually leave Greece. In 1949, the rabbi, his wife, and sons Joseph, Marius, and Yehoshua came to the United States. Here, the rabbi of Trikala became the rabbi of a Sephardic-Romaniote synagogue, Kehila Kedosha of Janina, in the South Bronx. His son Joseph, inspired by his father, teaches secular education as well as Torah, Jewish history, and the Holocaust.

ALBUM COVER

Made by Jerome Mahrer with cardboard from a Red Cross package. Tittmoning Internment Camp, Germany, 1943. Gift of Jerome and Carolyn Mahrer. While interned at Tittmoning, an internment camp for Americans, fourteen-year-old American-born Jerome created this cover for an album he compiled of sketches of fellow internees, drawn for him by an adult prisoner.

Mahrer Family

"Tell our boy that I played soccer again"

When Paul Mahrer proudly donned the broad red-striped jersey of the Czech national soccer team to represent his country in the 1924 Olympics in Paris, he could not have guessed that barely a generation later he would be a prisoner in his country's capital. In 1942, Mahrer was arrested and taken to the Gestapo prison in Karlplatz, in Prague.

Gifted with athletic ability, Paul Mahrer spent much of the 1920s and 1930s touring the world as a professional soccer player. He married Betty Gutmann, daughter of a distinguished Prague family whose relatives included singers, cantors, and even a friend of the great Czech Jewish writer Franz Kafka.

As an accomplished Jewish athlete, Mahrer frequently traveled abroad to play with the American Jewish teams, such as the Brooklyn Wanderers, in the HaKoah league of the New York metropolitan area. Teams with which Paul Mahrer was associated also played games and put on demonstrations in South and Central America.

Mahrer's son, Jerry, was born in the United States in 1929, giving him what would turn out to be lifesaving American citizenship. However, the depression forced the family to return to Prague in 1932, not long before the National Socialists' rise to power in neighboring Germany in 1933.

The German invasion and occupation of Czechoslovakia in March 1939 resulted in roundups and arrests of Jews, public humiliations, synagogue arson, compulsory registration, and confiscation of Jewish wealth and property. With the arrival of Adolf Eichmann in Prague in the summer of 1939, the pace of anti-Jewish measures increased dramatically.

Paul Mahrer's parents and extended family came to live near him after the German occupation. With the outbreak of war in September, however, arrests and de-

Photograph of Jerome Mahrer standing in front of his house. Prague, Czechoslovakia, March 1941. Gift of Jerome and Carolyn Mahrer.

portations of prominent Jews began. Mahrer's parents were eventually taken to Terezin, the garrison town near Prague, which had been converted by the Nazis into a "model" ghetto. Here, among others, many of the notable Jews from Germany, Austria, and Czechoslovakia were imprisoned—the wealthy, the famous, World War I veterans, and those well-connected Jews whom the Nazis might want to preserve, at least for now, for barter, bargaining, or ransom.

Throughout this accelerating crisis, Paul Mahrer played soccer for a well-known German club in Prague. He refused to wear the compulsory Jewish badge, the yellow star, and got away with this because of his "Aryan" appearance. However, mass deportations began in November 1941, and the Mahrer family was caught in the Nazi net.

Photograph of Paul Mahrer in a soccer uniform. Prague, Czechoslovakia. Gift of Jerome and Carolyn Mahrer.

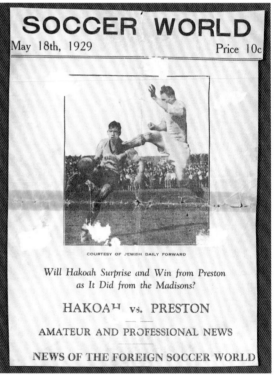

Cover of *Soccer World,* May 18, 1929. Gift of Jerome and Carolyn Mahrer. During the 1920s Paul Mahrer traveled often while playing soccer with a HaKoah team. He is shown here (on the right) on the cover of *Soccer World.*

In 1942, Paul Mahrer was arrested and sent to Terezin after a year in a Gestapo prison in Prague. The Nazi terror then closed around other family members. In May 1943, Mahrer's sons, Jerry and Peter, were arrested. Because of Jerry's American citizenship, they were taken to an internment camp in the castle at Tittmoning, in Germany. The following day, Betty Mahrer was also arrested. Although not an American citizen like her sons, Betty Mahrer was interned at Biberach, a camp for American women in Liebenau, Germany; Nazi logic insisted that she be in the same type of facility as her children, who were minors.

Tittmoning, where the Mahrer boys were sent, was a camp that housed American citizens, including a number of African American boxers and several musicians, such as jazz pianist Freddy Johnson. These performers, marooned by World War II in Europe, befriended Jerry Mahrer, who, at age thirteen, was the youngest internee. He became the camp "mascot," and in his rounds created an album of cartoon sketches of prisoners and guards, drawn by one of the prisoners.

The Jewish internees, targets of anti-Semitism in the camp, were segregated from the others, while the Nazis also separately segregated the black prisoners. The Mahrer boys had mail contact with their mother via the Red Cross but not with their father in Terezin. Paul Mahrer worked in the camp kitchen there and was allowed limited mail contact with his wife. Severely censored, Paul Mahrer's postcards from Terezin demonstrate how the writer was compelled to say that conditions were good—in effect to lie about the true conditions—or risk losing writing privileges in the future. However, the cards still convey Mahrer's love for his family, his pride in his sons, and in the athlete's profession. "We have enough. Tell our boy that I played soccer again and even played well and was successful. My beloved, just stay healthy and well. I love you. Kisses . . ."

In February 1945, Jerry and Peter were reunited with their mother and put on a train bound for Switzerland. They were part of an exchange for German POWs. Assembled from their various camps, the internees traveled through Switzerland to the French border. There, American soldiers escorted them to Marseille, where they sailed on a Swedish ship, arriving in New York two weeks later. When Terezin was liberated by the Soviets in May, Paul Mahrer was among the seventeen thousand Jews still alive there. He was able to join his family in New York a year later.

Mahrer Family

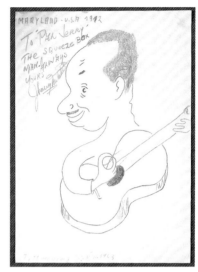

Drawings from Jerome Mahrer's album. Tittmoning Internment Camp, Germany, 1943. Gift of Jerome and Carolyn Mahrer. Fellow prisoner Max Brandl would sketch the prisoners for Jerome in exchange for cigarettes. The prisoners would then sign the sketches. Seen above is a profile of one of the many African American musicians who were interned in the camps, as well as a satiric profile of a German officer.

BOOK OF ESTHER

Handwritten megillat Esther on parchment, read by Rabbi Leo Baeck in the Terezin Ghetto, Czechoslovakia. Collection of Rabbi David Lipman. The Book of Esther is read on Purim. In Terezin, the Nazis forbade Jews to celebrate holidays, but ghetto residents often observed them in secret.

Rabbi Leo Baeck
Purim in Terezin

Rabbi Leo Baeck, one of the leaders of the German Jewish community, had been given opportunities to leave Germany, but he insisted on staying with his people. He was arrested twice by the Nazis for his attempts to defend the rights of the Jewish community. When he was deported to the Terezin Ghetto, near Prague, in 1943, his faith and that of many other religious Jews was severely tested.

In Terezin, Rabbi Baeck continued as a spiritual leader, speaking frequently to fellow inmates on religious and philosophical subjects. After hours of hard forced labor, Rabbi Baeck would often teach classes in order to keep inmates' minds active. His eloquence, demeanor, commanding physical presence, and firm ethical example in the midst of evil and brutality made a major contribution to the morale of the ghetto population.

When Red Cross officials came to Terezin to inquire about the condition of Jewish internees, the Nazis prepared for the visit with the full arsenal of their propaganda machine. Their plan was to deceive the world about their genocidal intent, presenting Terezin as a model city for privileged Jews, including World War I veterans and the elderly. The ruse included erecting false storefronts and even shooting a film featuring active, smiling prisoners. The truth was that the ghetto functioned as a concentration camp, serving as a transit facility to the death camp of Auschwitz. The year before Rabbi Baeck arrived, almost sixteen thousand people had died in Terezin of malnutrition, typhus, and other diseases. Constant hunger, poor sanitation, harsh labor, and daily brutalities prevailed.

Terezin was the opposite of a paradise, and yet a kind of miracle of faith and humanity unfolded there. Rabbi Baeck and other leaders helped organize a rich cultural life. Small rooms in some of the barracks were set up as synagogues, where Rabbi Baeck and others presided over religious services on Sabbath and holidays, and even for bar mitzvahs. These rituals were of enormous personal and communal importance during the Holocaust.

In a hidden bunker beneath a trapdoor, Rabbi Baeck celebrated Purim in the traditional manner by reading from the scroll, or megillah, of Esther. This biblical text tells the story of the courageous and beautiful Queen Esther, who persuades Ahasuerus, a king of ancient Persia, to reverse his genocidal minister Haman's plan to annihilate the Jews of his kingdom. The megillah's story of the ultimate rescue of the Jews of ancient Persia was a message the Terezin inmates suffering under the Nazis could translate into their own terms.

When the Soviet army finally liberated Terezin on May 8, 1945, approximately nineteen thousand of the one hundred forty thousand Jews deported there remained alive, but they were suffering from terrible weakness and disease. Maintaining his compassion for all human beings, Rabbi Baeck was influential at this time in restraining his fellow inmates from desperate acts of revenge on the Nazis.

But the story does not end here. Rabbi Baeck was evacuated to London to join the few surviving members of his family. Six weeks after the liberation of Terezin, Rabbi Eugene Lipman, an American army chaplain, arrived at the ghetto with the troops who were ordered to dismantle it.

"My father was leaving with the final truck," said Rabbi Lipman's son, David, remembering the story he had heard, "when one of the survivors asked him to wait. He went into the bunker and brought out the megillah and gave it to my father." Rabbi Lipman was asked to convey the sacred scroll to Rabbi Baeck.

When Rabbi Lipman found Rabbi Baeck in London, he offered him the scroll. Leo Baeck gave it back, stating that he no longer had a congregation. "I am giving it to you to make sure it will be read every year."

Rabbi Lipman honored Rabbi Baeck's request at his synagogue in the Washington, D.C., area, where he served from 1945 to 1987. When he retired, he passed the megillah along to his son, David, also a rabbi, who has used it with his congregation.

The megillah is on exhibition at the Museum eleven months of the year. However, every Adar, the Hebrew month in which Purim falls, the scroll is returned to Rabbi Lipman's congregation to be read. As the text is publicly chanted, congregants hear what happened in ancient Persia but are also reminded of what occurred in Terezin between 1941 and 1945.

Photograph of Rabbi Leo Baeck. Courtesy of the Leo Baeck Institute, New York.

Rabbi Lipman has said, "It has to be handed down to the next rabbi," who will also read it in front of his congregation. By doing this, he honors the oral agreement made between his father and Leo Baeck more than half a century ago, ensuring that the megillah read in Terezin continues to be read out loud on Purim.

Photograph of Rabbi Leo Baeck with Professor and Mrs. Martin Buber. Baeck and Buber were of the same generation of philosophical theological thinkers from German-speaking lands. Gift of Carol Biermann.

COMMUNION PHOTOGRAPH

Denise Feiler at her First Communion. Seiches, France, May 18, 1944. Gift of Denise Feiler Bensaid. Denise's mother was able to find a hiding place for Denise and her sister, Paulette, in a village in the Loire Valley, with a French Catholic family. The family and the village priests decided to baptize the girls after they learned of the death of their mother.

Denise (Dora) Feiler Bensaid
The Dreaded Day Arrived

Dora and Paulette Feiler and their little brother, Michel, were all born in Paris and proud of it. However, their parents, Beirel Feiler and Roche Leja Gimelstein, from Russia and Lithuania, respectively, were not French citizens. Fleeing their home countries because of persecutions and pogroms, they were among the tens of thousands of foreign Jews—economic immigrants and refugees who had entered France from eastern Europe.

Their small apartment building in the 18th Arrondissement was crowded with other proud, hardworking Jewish immigrant families like their own. This created a sense of community and, in the Feiler family, a commitment to observing Jewish holidays and customs. However, with the surrender of France to Germany in June 1940, Dora and Paulette began to sense a growing fear in their parents. Their parents were aware that as foreign Jews they would be especially vulnerable and likely the first targets of Nazi racial hatred, less protected by the French authorities.

It began almost immediately.

Under the terms of the armistice ratifying France's surrender, the country was divided into two zones: an occupied zone controlled by the Germans, with Paris as its hub, and an unoccupied zone that included much of the south, headed by the nominally "free" but collaborationist government of France, in the resort city of Vichy, near Bordeaux. From both centers of power, anti-Jewish laws and measures were enthusiastically promulgated.

During the early months of the occupation, Dora and Paulette, who were six and seven years old, were away for the summer at a country farm near Le Mans. By the time they returned to Paris, the German military administration and the Vichy government had already, among many other measures, revoked the law banning anti-Semitic articles in the French press and began requiring the stamping of

Photograph of Roche Leja Gimelstein. Paris, France, January 11, 1930. Gift of Denise Feiler Bensaid.

"Juif" (Jew) on identity cards and the posting of placards identifying Jewish shops. By October 1940, the government adopted the Statut des Juifs, which excluded Jews from public life.

Beirel Feiler was picked up in early 1941 with one hundred others. Among other eastern European Jewish immigrants, Feiler was active in an arm of the French resistance fighting Nazism. He participated in numerous actions against the enemy, notably in May 1941 when he deposited a bomb on rue Martel in Paris in a stock of winter jackets destined for the German army. In her husband's absence, and with his ultimate fate unknown, Roche Leja began to fear whether she could manage on her own. She was embarrassed by her accent and had Dora and Paulette do what shopping Jews were still permitted to do. The baby, Michel, had been born in July 1940.

The family huddled around the radio hoping for good news, but it did not come. Toward the end of 1941, French police, on their own or supervised by German soldiers, rounded up thousands more Jewish men. Feiler was among the group taken to the transit camp of Drancy, in a suburb northeast of Paris. Then a package with a note arrived at the family's apartment. Madame Feiler opened the note and read that her husband, Beirel Feiler, had been shot at Mont Valerien on December 15. He was dead. The package contained his effects: a spoon, a fork, a tin plate, and a tin cup.

The girls sensed that their mother was on the verge of collapse. Yet they had underestimated her. Roche Gimelstein Feiler now gathered herself to accomplish her next major goal: to find places to send her children into hiding. Like thousands of other desperate Jewish parents, she turned to the small but sympathetic element in the French population willing to help Jews. A Catholic neighbor, dressmaker Madame Jacob, assisted Madame Feiler in finding shelter for the girls. To increase the odds that someone in the family would survive, the Feiler girls were separated from their younger brother, Michel, who stayed with his mother. Dora and Paulette were sent to live in the home of a Catholic family, Mr. and Mrs. Branchereau, in a small village, seiches sur le Loir Maine et Loire.

The place was quiet and beautiful, but Dora was young enough to hope it was temporary and that she would soon return to Paris. Without her mother, her adjustment was particularly difficult, especially in school, where Paulette outshone her, fit in socially, and became popular. Dora, on the other hand, had grown awk-

Photograph of Dora (Denise) Feiler (four) and Paulette (five) in a school play. Paris, France, circa 1938. Collection of Paulette Feiler Goldstein.

wardly tall: she felt unloved in the family, and she tried to assuage her sense of loss by taking long walks alone in the fields. A peaceful feeling would come over her as she cherished her connection to nature.

Although numerous hidden Jewish children in France and throughout Europe had not only their lives protected but their Judaism respected, this, unfortunately, was not the case with the girls. One of the nuns in the school began to give Dora private religious lessons. In her loneliness, Dora became devoted to the worship of the Virgin Mary. The nun told her that if she continued to pray to the Virgin and to be good, her mother would come back. There was some solace for Dora in this belief, but also a powerful conflict, for Dora also knew she was Jewish and was attached to this identity.

Life became suddenly even harsher. Money that had regularly arrived by mail to support Dora and Paulette ceased. One day in 1943, the nuns and priests called Dora and Paulette into an office and told them that their mother "was not here anymore." In fact, she had been arrested, deported, and killed at the Majdanek

Photograph of Denise Feiler (ten), Paulette (eleven), and Michel (five) during a visit to their uncle. Paris, France, circa 1944. Collection of Paulette Feiler Goldstein.

Photograph of Paulette Feiler (thirteen) and Denise (twelve) [third row, first and third from the right] at a Jewish orphanage in Andrésy, France, circa 1946. Marc Chagall [top, center] visited the orphanage to help raise money. Collection of Paulette Feiler Goldstein.

death camp. The girls were told that now, in their mother's absence, they were finally ready to be baptized.

Dora was baptized as Denise, and never used the name Dora again. She saw the act of becoming a Christian as a way to keep praying even harder for the return of her mother. She went to communion and to masses, and she prayed to the Virgin to see her family once again. In time, it was a group of tall, handsome American soldiers who arrived, liberating the girls in 1945. As Denise remembered them, it was as if these liberators had arrived from another planet.

The girls were delighted to discover that their little brother, Michel, had survived. The three children, however, were not destined to live together. From 1947 to 1949, Michel was in a children's home in Aix-les-Bains. Thanks to an invitation from relatives in New York, Denise and Paulette were able to immigrate to America in 1949. Michel remained in France.

The girls struggled in America, but in time, life began to get a little better. Paulette sent her sister to beauty school, and Denise became a hairdresser. She met a French Protestant; they married and moved to Paris, where Denise was eager to integrate into French life. "I wanted to be French and nothing else," recalled Denise.

But when her first son was born, Denise suddenly felt very strongly that she no longer wanted to deny her Judaism. She had her son circumsised and began to feel that she was no longer lying to herself. Her marriage broke up, while her connection to Judaism was reborn. Memories of the apartment in the 18th Arrondissement came flooding back: the waxy warmth of the Sabbath candles and the aromas of the family dinners her mother used to prepare.

Returning to New York with her son, she met and married a French Algerian Jew and began to reconnect with her earlier life, reestablishing the sense of belonging that had been shattered when the Nazis marched into Paris. Denise now has four grandchildren, one of whom is named after her mother and one after her father, the Russian Jewish immigrant, who is honored at the memorial to the resistance at Mont Valerien, the fort outside Paris that was once used as Gestapo headquarters and where many resistance fighters were executed.

Denise (Dora) Feiler Bensaid

PATCHWORK DRESS

Dress worn by Sala Stein while hiding in Biecz, Poland, 1942–1945. Collection of the Stein Family. Sala Stein and her son, Shabtai, were hidden together on a farm for twenty-nine months. Sala would patch her one dress with whatever fabric was available. The original fabric was the black background with tiny colored flowers seen around the collar area.

Sala and Shabtai Stein

A Hidden Patchwork

Shabtai Stein knew well every single one of the many multicolored patches on his mother Sala's dress. The dress had not always been patched. It was made out of fine fabric with a black background and even had flowers on the collar. It was the dress she constantly wore during the nearly two and a half years that she and Shabtai were hiding from the Nazis in the woods near their hometown of Biecz, Poland.

Shabtai was eight years old in 1942 when the Nazis drove their trucks into Biecz one night. It was an *aktion,* a roundup, to capture and deport the town's small Jewish population. His mother and grandparents turned off the lights in their large house, which faced the town square. This time, they were lucky. They remained undetected in the basement for five days—with little water, food, or air. Shabtai was terrified. On the fifth day, the family frantically made their way past the barracks that had been turned into a ghetto, which already held hundreds of captured Jews awaiting deportation.

They were able to pass undetected into the woods. They kept moving, begging for water and food along the way. Many peasants in the forest refused, for helping Jews to evade the Germans often meant risking death. Finally, however, they arrived at the home of Alfonse Setlik, a Polish peasant known to some to be willing to provide shelter, and he agreed to let the Stein family hide on his property.

There were several hiding places—usually in holes beneath the floors of buildings used for the animals. At first, they were hidden in a stable, and then beneath the floor of the small granary. Animal excrement and urine often dripped down. Sala Stein's mother, hidden at another location, could no longer endure the conditions. She made her way into town, back to the house where she had been born, only to discover that a Polish family had expropriated it. The police were called. They asked her where her daughter, grandson, and the rest of the family were hiding. The police did not believe her when she said they were dead; she was taken away and shot.

Hidden away, changing locations, leaving the Setlik farm altogether every few months when people began to talk and they feared betrayal, Shabtai was continually scared and disoriented. His mother patched his primitive clothing and her own dress time and time again. There was little food, and he had no friends, toys, or books. The little boy was always afraid, too young to understand the full horror of what it was he feared. Although only eight years old, Shabtai's strong desire to live kept him going.

The hiding, but not the deprivation, came to an end in the spring of 1945 when the Red Army liberated the area. Sala Stein emerged wearing her dress of many patches. She and Shabtai were assigned by the Soviets to a room in the house they had been in when the deportations had begun twenty-nine months before. Food was still very scarce, as was clothing, but at least they were free and alive. Much of the family, however, had perished. An aunt and her children on Shabtai's father's side had survived. Only an aunt and grandfather on his mother's side could be found. Shabtai's father could not be traced and was presumed dead.

Photograph of Sala Stein holding her young son, Shabtai. Poland, circa 1936. Collection of Abraham Stein.

Photograph of Shabtai Stein and other children in a Jewish orphanage after the war. He was in the home for about one year. Stein is seated in the front row, third from the right. Bielsko, Poland, circa 1946. Collection of Abraham Stein.

For a time, they lived in a communal house in Biecz, and later Shabtai spent two years in orphanages. Finally, in 1947, Sala and Shabtai boarded a boat in Marseille bound for South America. Arriving in Bolivia, Shabtai was thirteen years old and still needed to complete elementary school, which he did. In the late 1950s, Shabtai Stein moved to Lima, Peru, where he met his wife, married, and became the father of two children.

To these grandchildren, Sala Stein gave the dress that she has kept all these years. "A special gift," she said. "Your inheritance."

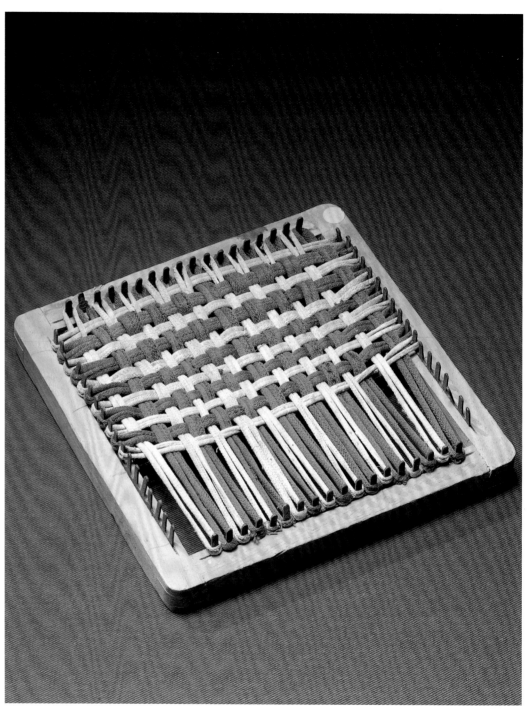

POTHOLDER ON TOY LOOM

Belonged to Yocheved Farber, Vilna Ghetto, Poland. Yaffa Eliach Collection, donated by the Center for Holocaust Studies. Yocheved Farber was three years old when the Germans occupied Vilna. She did not survive the war.

Kalman Farber and Family

"*There are holy things we simply do not understand*"

Erev Shavuot, the evening of the Feast of Weeks, 1942. There has been a special find, for today I procured some fish. I camouflaged them in the usual way, wrapping them in rags and hiding them on my body. Then I headed back to the ghetto."

So begins one of the entries in the extraordinary diary of Kalman Farber, a rabbinical student in Vilna, who with his wife, Zipporah, and three-year-old daughter, Yocheved, struggled to survive the occupation of the Nazis, which began on June 24, 1941. When Russian troops liberated Vilna on July 13, 1944, of the city's 57,000 Jews, 2,000 to 3,000 had survived, including the Farbers. Their daughter, Yocheved, however, was not with them. She had been abducted in a children's *aktion,* one of the roundups periodically organized by the Nazis to eliminate a portion of the population and to terrorize those who remained alive. Yocheved had been taken away and murdered.

Here is how Farber recorded that staggering event in his diary entry of March 27, 1944: "On this day, the children of Israel were taken from H. K. P. Camp . . . among them our Yocheved. . . . There are holy things we simply do not understand until a time in the future when God, blessed be He, might explain them to us."

Such sustained, profound faith in the face of tragedy was not an isolated instance in the Vilna Ghetto and elsewhere during the Holocaust. Kalman Farber and thousands of Orthodox Jews resisted dehumanization out of a conviction that nothing in the Nazi arsenal of terror would deter them from trying to live the daily life of observant Jews.

In the Farber family, this took the form of observing the Sabbath and the festivals, praying regularly, and, perhaps most daunting, maintaining kashrut, the

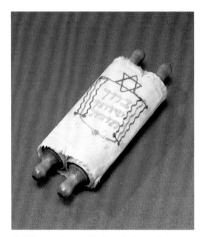

Child's torah scroll that belonged to Yocheved Farber. Vilna Ghetto, Poland. Yaffa Eliach Collection, donated by the Center for Holocaust Studies. Embroidered on the cover of the Torah scroll, in Hebrew, is: "Blessed is He who has given us the Torah."

exacting Jewish dietary laws, under conditions of mounting starvation, daily brutality, and death.

"Rosh Hashanah 1943 is nearing. There is pouring rain without letup. The cold is unbearable, and getting worse. Yet on the sixth floor of Block 2 we arranged for a place for prayers. We had a cantor and a shofar blower and also a Sefer Torah—a treasure from the ghetto. There was no shortage of people to say kaddish [the prayer said by mourners]."

On October 4, 1943, the day before Yom Kippur, Farber did not eat the soup prepared for all the workers, because it was not kosher. He refused to return to the camp from the work site by truck because he did not want to be riding when the holiday started.

From their apartment in Vilna, Kalman Farber had brought Yocheved's miniature Sefer Torah. It was the kind children carry and dance with on Simchat Torah, the holiday for the conclusion of the reading of the Torah; in 1943, it was celebrated on October 23. In the spring, he prepared the camp kitchen for Passover and baked matzot, the unleavened bread required for that festival. Each mitzvah (commandment) fulfilled was an assertion of will, dignity, and Jewish identity.

For the Farbers, religious observance went hand in hand with other acts of defiance and spiritual resistance. Since the Nazis deliberately provided Jews a ration insufficient to sustain life, smuggling of food was essential to survival. It was often necessary to try to find and bring in not only the special foods required by a holiday but also any food at all—peas, flour, beans—in order to survive. For Kalman Farber and his family, mere survival without remaining faithful to their religion was not an option.

Farber frequently wore a smuggling bag, specially sewn and fitted inside the leg of his trousers. When he returned to the ghetto from town, where he had bartered jewelry or other valuables for food, he was always at risk of being beaten by the Lithuanian police or German soldiers at the gate. More than once, he was caught, intimidated, and then ordered to strip down to his underwear and to lay out on the table what he and his fellow smugglers had managed to obtain: "The German smells the butter and asks the Lithuanian if it's fresh. Then he takes the fish for himself. After each item they take from us, they ask, 'Don't you have anything else, Jew?' Then they hit us with murderous blows. We left that place beaten up, wounded, and the financial loss was great too. But none of this deterred us, we were by no means broken, and we knew we would be going out again. As we used to say to each other, 'as long as your head is in one piece, then you need to keep going out tomorrow.'"

Having liquidated nearly all the Jews remaining in the Vilna Ghetto as the Soviets approached in the summer of 1944, the Germans targeted for annihilation all the remaining workers in the H.K.P. (a military garage for the repair of German vehicles) and other forced labor camps near Vilna. Farber and his wife made several unsuccessful attempts to escape. Finally, they were able to find a *maline* in the Vilna Ghetto, one of many hiding places fashioned out of chimneys, cupboards, and ovens, in basements. On July 4, 1944, the Jews remaining in the H.K.P. were rounded up and taken to the nearby forest of Ponary. About six miles from Vilna, this was the site where tens of thousands of the Jews of Vilna had already been executed. Now, the remainder of the Jewish population of Vilna, once known for its vital Jewish life, was forced into pits and shot. Kalman and Zipporah Farber in their *maline* in the empty ghetto had evaded evacuation to Ponary and this fate.

Having managed to elude the last roundups, the Farbers fled the ghetto as the Germans were blowing up the evidence and as the guns of the liberating Soviet army neared. When he left the area of the Vilna Ghetto for the last time, Kalman Farber was carrying with him a copy of the Book of Psalms and, in the other pocket, a pair of tefillin, or phylacteries. He and Zipporah were among the first of many Holocaust survivors to settle in Palestine.

Photograph of Yocheved Farber (about two years old) in the resort town of Druskeniki (near Vilna) on July 10, 1939. Yaffa Eliach Collection, donated by the Center for Holocaust Studies.

TRUMPET

Played by Louis Bannet in the men's orchestra at Birkenau death camp, Poland. Gift of Louis Bannet. Known in Holland as the "Dutch Louis Armstrong," Bannet played for more than two years in the Birkenau inmate orchestra and owes his life to his trumpet.

Louis Bannet
"I played for my life"

During the 1920s and 1930s, the clever dancing melodies of Louis's Rhythm Five and the jazzy riffs of Louis Bannet and His Adventurers helped to establish Louis Bannet's reputation as one of the most celebrated trumpeters in all of Europe—the "Dutch Louis Armstrong."

However, the story of Louis Bannet and of the trumpet that saved his life in Auschwitz-Birkenau begins with a violin. Rotterdam-born Louis Bannet began to play the violin at age seven, his studies supported by the Dutch Jewish communal organization. At age fourteen, he went to a music store to buy a new instrument so he could play jazz. The thirty guilders he had borrowed, however, weren't enough for the saxophone he craved; but a trumpet was affordable.

Bannet was a natural, and with time he formed and led several groups and helped popularize American jazz in Europe. Through performance and publicity photographs, his face became well known. He even once played before the queen of Holland. Yet all this came to a rapid end when the Germans conquered and then occupied Holland in May 1940. When the "Jews Are Not Permitted" signs began to appear in club and hotel windows, Louis had to quit. He went into hiding with a member of the Dutch underground in June 1942.

Within six months, however, he was recognized in a baker's shop in the small town of Drimmelen, where he was arrested at gunpoint. On a train with 635 members of the Dutch underground, he was deported to Auschwitz. There, the Dutch interpreter for the Germans recognized him. He was told he might audition for the Men's Orchestra of Birkenau, one of the camp's orchestras and bands. If Louis Bannet's playing pleased a man named Franz Kopka, the virulently anti-Semitic Ukrainian *kapo* of the music detail, his life might be spared—for a while.

His fame, which had previously betrayed him, was giving Louis Bannet, now known as prisoner number 93626, a chance to survive. Bannet described the bitter winter morning of his audition:

> Two of my comrades, a trombonist and saxophonist, were with me. . . . It was terribly cold. . . . There was a fat, ugly-looking Ukrainian in the room. His name was Kopka. He was the *kapo* of the music detail . . . Auschwitz prison's 42-piece band. . . . I wondered if any music could touch his soul. If he had a soul. I picked out this trumpet from the assortment of instruments. I never felt less like playing, and I hoped I wouldn't be first. . . . The trombonist was the first man to play. I had played with him, and I knew he was a good musician. But his music didn't please the Ukrainian, who waved him out. It wasn't a fair test. There was a stove in this room, and I got near enough to it so I could warm my fingers and rub them over my lips. My turn came next.
>
> I started to play "St. Louis Blues." American jazz had become very popular in Europe, and this tune was very well known. I kept my eyes on the Ukrainian's face while I played, and God help me if he didn't like my music. . . . It was the most important concert of my life.

Louis Bannet played music at Birkenau for more than two years. During this period, many of the 1.3 million who walked toward their deaths in the Birkenau gas chambers heard his music on the way. "You couldn't open your mouth. You couldn't go near," he recalled. "A dog is more than you are when you are a number." Most of Bannet's forty-one family members were killed by the Nazis at Auschwitz-Birkenau, including his sisters and their children.

He was, however, able to save the life of his older brother, who had weakened and was unable to work. That was a death sentence. Bannet hid his brother in a cart full of refuse that the band hauled away each day, and then sneaked him past the guards to a storeroom, where he smuggled in medicine and brought him back to health. His brother survived.

In November 1944, as the Allies neared, the SS began marching the surviving inmates out of Auschwitz. With his trumpet tied around his waist with a rope, Bannet arrived at the camp at Ohrdruf, Germany. Here, there was no orchestra, only backbreaking manual labor. When he found time to sleep, he wrapped the trumpet in a cloth and used it for his pillow.

Exhausted, Bannet was about to give up, when a friend came to the rescue. He introduced him to a music-loving SS officer, who presented Bannet with a violin

Publicity photograph of Louis Bannet with his trumpet. Holland, 1938. Gift of Louis Bannet.

with only two strings on it. Here was another test. Thinking fast, Louis played "My Home Is a Star," a sentimental German melody. The SS man started to cry; he called his wife on the phone and had Bannet play the tune for her. Bannet was shaved and allowed to clean up, and then he played the tune for every SS officer in the camp. Once again, music had given him power—along with extra food for survival.

As the Soviets came nearer, Louis Bannet endured more concentration camps—Sachsenhausen and then Buchenwald, where he was one of 51,000 prisoners transported there by the Nazis as the Allies advanced. He was again moved out, this time onto a train, where he spent more than a month with 103 people. Many died each day from typhus. Finally liberated in May 1945, Louis Bannet was one of 17 of the 103 people to survive this final train ride.

He returned to Holland, where he eventually formed a new band and played throughout Belgium, Switzerland, and France. When he finally settled in Canada with his family, Louis Bannet still had his trumpet with him.

INMATE CAP
Worn by Hanoch Kolman at Auschwitz-Birkenau death camp, Poland, 1943–1944. Gift of Henry Coleman. Kolman was deported to Auschwitz in November 1942. When his uniform cap became worn, a friend in the camp made this one—unusual because it is lined for warmth.

Henry Coleman
The Cap of Hanoch Kolman

The cap that Hanoch Kolman wore as a prisoner at Auschwitz-Birkenau in the bitter winters of 1942 and 1943 was, in many ways, quite ordinary. Naturally, it did what any cap was designed to do: it fit snugly around his shaved head, and it provided some warmth. He wore it as he worked repairing the bricks at the ovens, which were constantly cracking from overuse, at the Auschwitz-Birkenau crematoriums.

What made the blue-and-beige-striped cap really exceptional was that there was a lining inside that diminished the life-threatening loss of body heat. Yet what was truly wonderful about the cap is that it was made for Hanoch Kolman by a friend when his original one, the thin, standard-issue Nazi cap, had deteriorated. Such kindness, often undertaken at great personal risk and sacrifice, not only preserved lives but also helped to shore up the sense of humanity and dignity of both giver and receiver. This gesture was particularly significant at Auschwitz-Birkenau, the largest and most deadly of the Nazi killing centers.

When the war came to Hanoch Kolman in his small town of Rypin, in north central Poland, not far from the Vistula River, which runs north into the Gulf of Danzig, he was not quite fifteen and a half years old. He was active in the pioneering Jewish youth movement, Hashomer Hatzair, a Zionist group inspired by socialist values and Jewish nationalism.

The second youngest of six children—his oldest brother was a soldier in the Polish army—Hanoch had just received a scholarship on the eve of the war, to attend an agricultural school whose goal was to send its students to work as farmers in Palestine.

Trying to evade the Germans, Kolman and several of his siblings eventually fled to Włocławek, on the eastern side of the Vistula. However, when the Germans began bombing this city, they returned to Rypin. There, they found not only that the Nazis had arrived, but that they had already shot the town's prominent Jews, including Hanoch's father. The Germans then transported the remaining Jews of Rypin to the nearby town of Mlawa, where a ghetto was set up in early December 1940. In an act designed to terrorize the community, the Germans burned down the Mlawa synagogue and all the synagogues in the vicinity.

For two years, Hanoch Kolman and his family lived in the Mlawa Ghetto under conditions of accelerating starvation, disease, and the sustained terror of continuing roundups and deportations. Kolman, however, was sent to forced labor at Nosarzewo, a labor camp twenty kilometers outside of Mlawa. Although conditions at the labor camp were also terrible, he was able to steal food with an eye to supplementing the meager rations being provided to his family. Yet how could he transport it back to the ghetto? Eventually, he was befriended by a German guard at Nosarzewo, who arranged for Kolman to be assigned work that permitted him to shuttle back and forth from the labor camp and to spend one night a week with his family.

When the Mlawa Ghetto was liquidated in November 1942, Hanoch Kolman and his sisters were deported to Auschwitz-Birkenau. His sisters were murdered there, but he managed to stay alive because he was chosen to be part of a group of young men who were to be taught bricklaying, a job that the Nazis considered vital; they especially needed these trainees to repair the cracked ovens at the crematoriums.

When he had first arrived at Auschwitz-Birkenau, Kolman was given the typical uniform—thin, striped coat, jacket, and pants—and also a cap, equally thin. After six months, when he was transferred to work in the nearby Birkenau death camp, his hat had become threadbare and badly deteriorated. It was here that he made a friend who worked in one of Birkenau's factories and who sewed a new cap for him. In Auschwitz, he also met his sister-in-law, Jean; at the time, neither of them knew that her husband, Hanoch's brother, had already been killed.

Finally liberated in February 1945 at Danzig, where he had been transported and forced to work repairing German submarines, Hanoch Kolman made his way back to Rypin. There he discovered his family's house was occupied by a Polish family, who at first refused to leave. He reconnected with his sister-in-law, Jean, whom he married in Rypin, and they eventually retrieved ownership of the house.

However, this was quite a hard-fought victory and a relatively unusual success, given the continuation of anti-Semitism in postwar Poland. In the confusing and chaotic months after the war, Kolman and his new bride decided to leave Rypin for the relative haven of the DP camps.

Through the assistance of Jewish organizations, such as the Hebrew Immigrant Aid Society (HIAS), the Kolmans were eventually able to immigrate to the United States. Through concentration camps and DP camps and for many years after, Hanoch Coleman (now Henry Coleman) kept that cap with him. It was a remnant and reminder of what he had lived through. When visitors view it at the Museum, they may begin to comprehend how the harshness that inmates endured in the concentration camps was mitigated—however slightly—by ingenuity and friendship.

Henry Coleman

BLOUSE

Hand-embroidered blouse made by Chaya Porus for her sister, Rachel. Gift of Simon and Chaya Palevsky. Sorting the belongings of those murdered at Ponary, a friend recognized the blouse Chaya Porus had made for her sister, Rachel, and gave it to Porus. She wore the blouse while she was in the forest with the partisans, as if to keep her sister close to her.

Palevsky Family
"As if I was carrying her close to me"

Flowers and leaves were embroidered on the front of her yellow blouse. It was thin and dainty. His sweater was unadorned, simple, and warm. Chaya Porus and Simon Palevsky kept these garments close to them. Porus's blouse belonged to her sister, Rachel. Palevsky's sweater was knitted for him, a gift from his wife, Rebecca. Rebecca and Rachel were dead, along with virtually all the other members of their families, which is why Chaya Porus took such good care of the garments. She darned them with a needle borrowed from a peasant and with silk threads from a Soviet parachute.

On a summer morning in 1943, deep in the Naroch Forest, ninety-three miles east of Vilna, then part of Lithuania, these articles of clothing and the memories they evoked allowed Porus and Palevsky to keep their families near to them. For Porus and Palevsky were Jewish partisans of the Nekama Brigade—Nekama in Hebrew means revenge—and they were about to move out on a mission to attack the Nazis.

Chaya Porus never thought she would be carrying a gun and a knife. The fourth of six children in a well-to-do Jewish family in Swieciany, near Vilna, twenty-one-year-old Porus had been hoping to go to medical school in Paris when the Germans occupied her town on June 24, 1941. Within a month, five thousand Jewish men were rounded up in *aktions,* or mass arrests, on the streets of Vilna, and sent seven miles away to the forest of Ponary for execution. The mass murder at Ponary was, at first, kept from the Jews of Vilna and its surrounding towns, such as Swieciany. But by the end of 1941, when the Germans had already killed 35,000 of Vilna's 57,000 Jews and, in addition, 2,500 Jews from Swieciany—with a total of 8,000 from other towns—the truth was out.

The Porus family joined the underground resistance in the Swieciany Ghetto.

Their large house was used to store ammunition, guns, and stolen machinery parts from a nearby airplane factory, materials that could be fashioned into guns. Porus's mother and her sister, Rachel—for whom Chaya had just made, as a birthday gift, a beautifully embroidered yellow blouse—packed the weapons to be smuggled out to the partisans in the forest. Chaya Porus was part of a group of Jewish students organized by Shieke Gertman to fight the Germans. Gertman was going to bring this Jewish group into the nearby forest to join Feodor Markov, one of their former teachers of Polish in the Swieciany high school. In February 1943, Markov began organizing Soviet soldiers into a partisan group to fight the Nazis. The question was when to make the break from the ghetto to the forest. To do so—to resist the Nazis in this particularly courageous way—was an agonizing moral crisis for the young people. For the Nazis exacted terrible reprisals on the families left behind by those who fled the ghetto.

Yet the Poruses were actively resisting as a family. When Chaya took sick with typhus, she was cared for by Rachel, a registered nurse who served in the ghetto's clandestine hospital. Chaya had not yet recovered when, in early April 1943, the remaining Jews of Swieciany were rounded up, including the Porus family. They were loaded on to cattle cars bound, allegedly, for the larger ghetto in Kovno. Each member of the Porus family carried a small bundle of personal possessions.

Chaya Porus was too weak to walk. She was ready to be carried on a stretcher to the deportation train, but her partisan friends insisted on taking her with them to Vilna. When they arrived there, they learned that the train from Swieciany had not gone to Kovno at all. Taking on, along the way, inhabitants of other smaller ghettos in the environs of Vilna—Mikaliskes, Oshmiany, and many more, with a combined total of 5,000 Jews—the train had traveled directly to Ponary, where all were herded into pits and shot.

Several days later, in Vilna, where the Swieciany partisans joined other partisan groups remaining in the ghetto, Chaya Porus, who had grown stronger, was handed a package by Luba Gurwitz, a friend of her sister's. Gurwitz's assignment during the last several days had been to sort through the clothes of those killed at Ponary. When Chaya opened the package, she found the bundle her sister had carried to Ponary; it included a towel, a coat, a photo album, and the embroidered blouse.

The group of partisans Porus now joined was part of the larger United Partisan

Organization (FPO in Yiddish) which was formed in January 1942 in response to Abba Kovner's call for armed resistance in the ghetto. The armed resistance young Jews now called for was a great challenge to the ghetto leadership, the Judenrat, which discouraged it, for such actions invited immediate and mass reprisals from the Nazis. The FPO, in turn, accused the Judenrat, which was responsible for maintaining Jewish life under impossible Nazi demands and providing work quotas for the Nazis, of unwittingly being the instrument of the Jews' incremental demise.

Porus's group escaped to the Naroch Forest in the late summer of 1943, joined the Markov partisans, and formed the Nekama Brigade, consisting of 200 Jewish fighters. A month later, on September 23 and 24, around the Jewish High Holidays—a time the Germans favored for such activities—the Nazis implemented the final liquidation of the 3,700 Jews still surviving in the Vilna Ghetto.

Porus met Simon Palevsky in the Markov partisan group, and the two grew close. The Jewish partisans in the forests around Vilna—and elsewhere—operated in the midst of a hostile and often anti-Semitic civilian population. They had also to contend with hostility and anti-Semitism from other partisan groups, including the Soviets, who had overall command of the partisan units. The Soviets often refused to let Jews form independent Jewish partisan units and were sometimes reluctant to accept Jews into their ranks.

Still, the partisans in Porus and Palevsky's group carried out daring missions. While they were under no illusions that they could actually vanquish the Nazis, they blew up bridges; attacked small patrols; destroyed train tracks, locomotives, and power supplies; and cut lines of communication.

The Markov partisan groups had fighting units and a working unit, which provided them with food. Nearby were a few Jewish family bunkers, where the children and elderly stayed. Porus had responsibilities in both units of the camp. At first, she went on military missions, but later she worked primarily nursing the wounded in the family camp that supported the fighters. She also often carried a gun and a knife. But what kept her whole was the love that was growing between her and Simon Palevsky even in the midst of the war.

When the Soviet army finally liberated the Naroch Forest, Chaya Porus and Simon Palevsky returned to Vilna, where they were married in the summer of 1944.

PREWAR PHOTOGRAPH OF RICHARD ROZENCWAJG
Richard Rozencwajg with his parents and other adults. Poland, April 16, 1939. Gift of Richard Rozen. Seen here (left to right) are Richard's mother, father, and maternal aunt. Richard's father, Pinkus, was a doctor who worked with Armia Krajowa partisans in a forest in Poland. This is the last photograph taken of Pinkus Rozen.

Richard Rozen

Feather Boy

Richard Rozencwajg was high in the air in the forest outside the city of Radom, Poland, where he had been born. During air raids, the trees could be surprisingly safe, although, of course, Richard would have preferred to shoot a gun. The partisans had trained him, but at eight years old, he just wasn't strong enough. He could shoot the gun only if his father or one of the partisans wedged it for him on stones or in the crotch of a sapling.

The problem was that his father was too busy to practice with him. His father was the partisans' doctor; he could not find the time to wedge the gun or, it seemed, to ever play with Richard. It was not easy, but the boy was coming to understand this. After all, it was the winter of 1943, deep in the forests, where the partisans had set up their secret medical unit, and they were at war.

Richard sensed that the partisans—a unit of Armia Krajowa (AK), the official Polish home army—who had rescued them from the Germans were not really fond of his father or himself. They were ordered around a lot. Richard certainly had heard the crude and cruel jokes, and he was old enough to know they weren't liked because they were Jews. Still, it didn't make much sense to Richard, because his father's apron was always covered with the partisan fighters' blood from all the work he did trying to keep them alive.

He felt safe enough, and he knew his mother was also safe and living in the nearby village. Richard had to be brave. Each man had a specific job to do in order to kill the Germans. Richard's father's job was to fix up the AK's men if they were wounded, so they could go out and fight against the Nazis. And Richard, too, had his work. He was the feather boy, and he was very proud of it.

Before he was feather boy, he had been just an ordinary boy. In 1939, when he was four years old, the Germans attacked Poland, and Richard and his parents

Photographs of Richard Rozen-cwajg as a young boy. Zwolen, Poland, 1938–1939. Gift of Richard Rozen.

90

fled east into Soviet territory. His father, Pinkus, became head of the military hospital at Lubomyl. When the Germans occupied Lubomyl, they humiliated his father by making him do the work of an orderly; then they forced all the Jews into the ghetto. But Richard's father had managed to save some money, and he used it to make an arrangement with a peasant couple.

The family left the ghetto by night in a wagon, and the peasants hid them in a wardrobe—a large closet—in the cellar of their house. In the closet, Richard could stand up and walk back and forth, but only if his parents moved to one side and lay close together. His mother, Rojza Szyfra, told him stories; his father taught him the alphabet and arithmetic by drawing the shapes of the letters and numbers in the palms of Richard's hands.

After twelve months, the family's money ran out. Richard's father appealed to the peasants to let them stay longer, and they agreed, for a price: one more month in exchange for the last valuable his father had left, a pair of fine French leather shoes.

A month later, the peasants evicted the Rozencwajg family, gave them a bag of food, and directed them to the partisans in the forest. These partisans, however, wanted all foreigners, which meant Jews along with Germans, out of Poland. They turned the Rozencwajg family over to the Gestapo, who immediately transported them to the ghetto in Lublin.

When other partisans—the Armia Krajowa—realized Richard's father was a physician, the family was smuggled out of the ghetto in a rag wagon. In exchange for his father's services, Richard and his mother were allowed to live in the village, while his father headed the partisan medical unit in the forest.

To alter his identity in order to protect him, Richard was dressed as a girl and presented as a sick child. Richard tried hard to be a girl, but it was not easy. It was difficult to switch speech patterns and word endings to feminine gender. It was odd also to try to walk like a girl. Although his mother showed him, it was particularly difficult to urinate like a girl. One did these things, she explained, in order to survive.

Yet why did the child not go to school? The partisans began to fear Richard and his mother would be recognized in the village as Jews. If they were turned over to the Germans, under torture they might betray the partisans' position. Richard's father would leave them, and they would again be without a doctor.

After three months of this masquerade, it was determined that Richard could not continue hiding in the village any longer. He had a tearful parting from his mother, and the partisans took him deep into the forest to the medical unit. For his eighth birthday, on April 15, 1943, he was given the best present he had ever received in his entire life: a whole loaf of Polish peasant bread all for himself.

At least Richard could now be near his father. The partisans also gave him an important job to do. They gave him a feather, which he kept in his belt. After each battle, Richard's job was to walk around and place the feather under the noses of the enemy bodies that were laying about. Richard had to hold the feather carefully, without any movement, under each nose while counting to one hundred. If the feather fluttered at all during that time, he was to call one of the partisans over, who then shot the German again, killing him.

During the second winter, the coldest and hardest, Richard was in a tree during a bombing raid. When the explosions stopped, he climbed down. There were no bodies to apply the feather to that he could see, but this time he noticed an entire human leg complete with a boot. The leg was just about as large as Richard. Without a second's hesitation, he went over to it and dragged it 200 meters in the snow all the way to the hospital where he knew his father was working.

Richard's father was wearing an apron stained with blood, like a butcher. When he saw the leg, his father took it and came as close to tears as Richard ever remembered. "But it's perfect," Richard said to him. "I thought you could use the leg to fix someone who had lost his own!" That was the last time he saw his father, who disappeared during a sudden German raid on the hospital.

When the Soviets liberated the forest, Richard and his mother returned to Radom. But the Poles threatened them and drove them away. Because Richard was ill, he spent time in a sanitarium for refugees. When he recovered, he and his mother moved through several Displaced Persons (DP) camps, arriving finally at the camp at Stuttgart, in Germany. Here he was given the only clothing that could be provided for the boys: Hitler Youth uniforms.

Eventually, Richard and his mother made their way to Paris, and then, in 1951, to Melbourne, Australia, to live with an uncle who had survived the war in Russia. Richard Rozen, as he would call himself, grew up, married, and raised a family. The war experiences as a hidden child had shaped his life in fascinating ways. He excelled at chess and bridge—games that are played in the confined spaces of a board and table and that require the memory work he engaged in with his father back in the peasants' wardrobe in the first winter of the war.

Richard and his mother looked for years for his father, but he had disappeared without a trace.

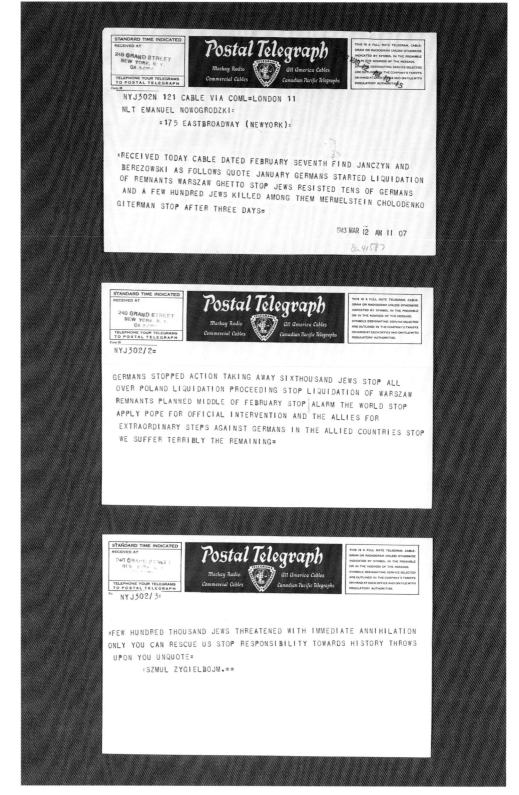

TELEGRAM

From Szmul Zygielbojm, Jewish Labor Bund representative in London, to the Bund offices in New York. London, England, March 12, 1943. Bund Archives. YIVO Institute for Jewish Research, New York. Struggling to rouse the world from its apathy, he reports the horrific murder of Poland's Jews and appeals to the Allies and the pope.

Szmul Zygielbojm

"I WAS UNABLE TO SAVE
A SINGLE ONE OF THEM STOP"

Szmul Zygielbojm was not a Jewish martyr in the usual sense of the term: he was not a zealot besieged by Romans, or a rabbi confronting conversion or the crusader's sword. Nor was he confronting deportation, as were his family and the thousands of others he had to leave behind in Poland.

Yet Zygielbojm's suicide on May 12, 1943, was far more than a personal act. It was also a desperate public moral gesture, unique in the history of the Holocaust, to call the world's attention to the accelerating annihilation of the Jewish people of Poland.

Born in Borowice, a village near Lublin, Zygielbojm went to work early in life and soon became a member of the Bund, one of the most important Jewish socialist labor organizations. By 1924, he was a key official of the Bund and secretary to the Central Council of Jewish Trade Unions. In the 1930s, Zygielbojm was organizing and leading the Bund branch in the industrial city of Lodz. His leadership extended beyond the Jewish community, and in 1938, he was elected to the Lodz City Council.

When World War II broke out, Zygielbojm was in Warsaw, where he was one of two Jewish leaders among a total of twelve hostages that the Germans took at the beginning of the occupation. All political parties were outlawed, but Zygielbojm, who was released, helped establish the Bund's underground activities in order to organize a response to the occupation. He was also chosen to represent the Bund in Warsaw's Judenrat.

In danger of being arrested again for his clandestine activities, he fled to Belgium in December 1939, where he reported to a Socialist International meeting: it was to be the first of many attempts to document the stages of the Nazi occupa-

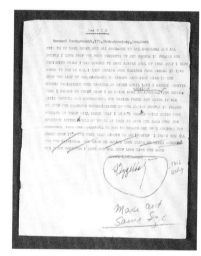

Original signed carbon copy of the English version of Zygielbojm's final protest, addressed to his comrades in the New York office of the Jewish Labor Bund. London, England, May 12, 1943. Bund Archives. YIVO Institute for Jewish Research, New York. Found on Zygielbojm's desk after his suicide, the letter is his last attempt to protest the world's lack of response to the Nazi slaughter of Europe's Jews.

tion of Poland and to alert the world to the accelerating persecution of the Jews. It was also personally wrenching for Zygielbojm to leave behind his family members, including his wife and son.

After Belgium fell to the Germans, Zygielbojm escaped to France, and in September 1940, he was sent to New York. In March 1942, Zygielbojm was sent to London as the Bund's representative and as a member of the National Council of the Polish government-in-exile. In these sensitive posts, he continued to receive information via secret courier and radio linkups to Bund members still surviving underground.

In May 1942, Zygielbojm released a report based on information sent to him from the Bund in Warsaw. It told of the murder of Polish Jews on a massive scale. This news, which became known as the Bund Report, was one of the first sources documenting the genocide of the Jews. It contained a list of cities, towns, and villages where roundups of the Jewish population had occurred. The report cited camps and other locations where Jews had been killed, and it estimated that seven hundred thousand Jews had already been killed.

Szmul Zygielbojm now dedicated himself completely to alerting the Western media to the gravity of the situation in Poland, and to the need for an immediate plan to rescue the remaining Jews. He campaigned with letters, telegrams, and speeches, including one address broadcast by the BBC on June 2, 1942; it stated in plain language that Jewish Poles were being singled out and killed on an unprecedented, organized, and massive scale.

In September 1942, he disclosed reports of the Polish government-in-exile that seven thousand Jews were being deported daily from Warsaw to their deaths. Zygielbojm was pinning his hopes in great part on the by-invitation-only Anglo-American conference that would take place in Bermuda in April 1943, an inaccessible venue that allowed the organizers to control the number of reporters and private Jewish organizations attending. Its aim was to provide if not a concrete plan then at least hope for the rescue of the remaining Jews of Poland. On March 12, 1943, Zygielbojm sent an urgent message to his Bund colleagues in New York:

ALL OVER POLAND LIQUIDATION PROCEEDING STOP . . . ALARM THE WORLD STOP APPLY THE POPE FOR OFFICIAL INTERVENTION AND THE ALLIES FOR EXTRAORDINARY STEPS . . . ONLY YOU CAN RESCUE US STOP RESPONSIBILITY TOWARD HISTORY THROWS UPON YOU SZMUL ZYGIELBOJM.

Photograph of Szmul Zygielbojm in Warsaw, Poland, December 7, 1927. Bund Archives. YIVO Institute for Jewish Research, New York.

The responsibility Zygielbojm felt he personally carried to save a remnant of the Polish Jewish community grew terrible to bear. In early May 1943, news arrived of the failure of the Bermuda conference to aid the Jews under the Nazis. It was followed soon after by a report of the crushing of the uprising in the Warsaw Ghetto. On May 12, Zygielbojm also received news that his wife, Manya, and his son were among those killed in the Germans' final liquidation of the ghetto.

In despair, Zygielbojm determined to take his own life. However, the letters of farewell that he now sat down to write—to his brother, his colleagues at the Polish Bund in New York, as well as to the president of the Polish government-in-exile—testify to the public dimension of his act. In his farewell letter to the Bund, he wrote:

> I am going away as a protest against the democratic nations . . . not having taken any steps at all to stop the complete extermination of the Jewish people in Poland. Perhaps my death will cause what I did not succeed while alive.

His last hope was to achieve in death what he had not achieved in life. He took a dose of sodium amatol and died, at age forty-six, alone in his London apartment. He was surrounded by the letters and telegrams designed for public distribution, and also by instructions that his body be cremated.

Szmul Zygielbojm's ashes were brought to New York by his Bund colleagues after the war, and he was honored in a formal ceremony at Carnegie Hall in 1961. The originals of Zygielbojm's letters and telegrams, which have been on exhibition at the Museum of Jewish Heritage—A Living Memorial to the Holocaust, courtesy of the YIVO Institute for Jewish Research, constitute a reminder of the catastrophic consequences when good people and good nations are unable to act in response to urgent and prophetic warnings.

Szmul Zygielbojm

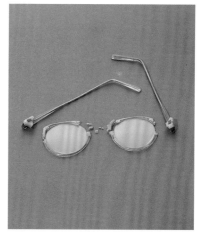

Eyeglasses used by Szmul Zygielbojm, found after his suicide in London, May 12, 1943. Bund Archives. YIVO Institute for Jewish Research, New York. Trained as a carpenter, Zygielbojm was a self-educated writer, editor, and speaker. He became an activist in socialist causes and an eloquent spokesman for Poland's Jews.

Business card listing Zygielbojm as a member of the Polish National Council, in Polish and English. London, England, 1942. Bund Archives. YIVO Institute for Jewish Research, New York. Zygielbojm's prominent position on the Polish National Council in London gave him a platform from which to speak out on behalf of Poland's Jews.

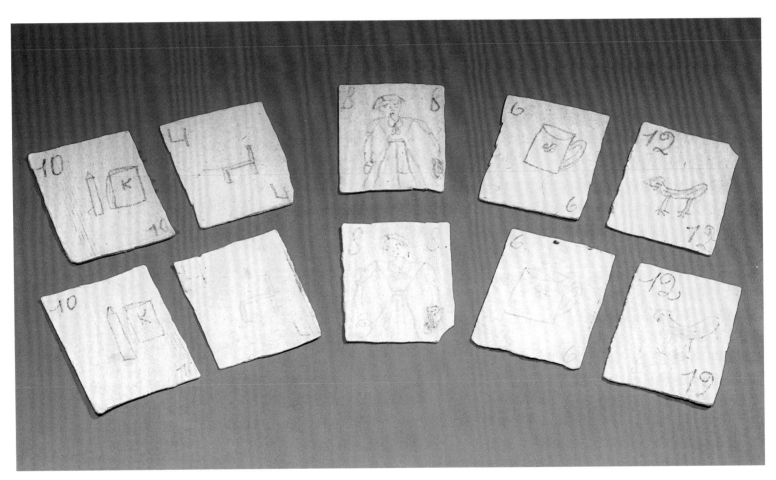

PLAYING CARDS

Made by Rose Silberberg, used with her sister, Mala, in hiding in a chicken coop. Sosnowiec, Poland, 1943. Gift of Rose Skier, Yaffa Eliach Collection, donated by the Center for Holocaust Studies. The Silberbergs, about to be deported, paid a Lithuanian woman to hide them. The SS found them in 1944. Only Rose escaped.

Rose Silberberg Skier
The Chicken Coop

Rose Silberberg decided to make the fours chairs, the sixes large-handled mugs, and the eights a strong, capable young woman with a part in her hair and wearing a long peasant dress. Maybe she was a little like her own pretty mother. Now what might the twelves be?

Nine-year-old Rose carefully drew two strutting chickens, complete with tail feathers and sharp little claws. The chicken drawing on the playing card was indeed perfect, for Rose knew full well she was hiding from the Nazis in Mrs. Chicha's chicken coop. When her four-and-a-half-year-old sister, Mala, began to sing, Rose quickly put her hand over her sister's mouth. For that sound of joy—any sound—might give away their hiding place.

They had not always lived so. In the city of Jaworzno, in southwestern Poland, the Silberbergs, descendants of a large Hasidic family, had been well-to-do enough for Rose to have a nursemaid, whom she occasionally accompanied to her church, without anyone knowing. Mala had a beautiful voice and loved to sing. Life was good for the Silberberg girls and their parents, Felicia and Moses, Aunt Sara, and the uncles and cousins who were always around.

With the occupation of Poland, the Silberbergs fled from their town to Sosnowiec, a city not far away. Then the Germans occupied Sosnowiec on September 4, 1939, and immediately attacked its 28,000 Jewish residents. Within five days, they had burned down the synagogue, issued severe restrictions on personal behavior, and expropriated Jewish property. The Jewish community was herded into a ghetto created in Srodula, one of the poorest neighborhoods of Sosnowiec. The Nazis forced the Judenrat, the Jewish council, to provide labor for the coal and iron mines and other industries in the area. By August 18, 1942, after an *aktion,* or roundup, 11,500 people had been sent to various forced labor camps or to nearby Auschwitz-Birkenau to be murdered.

Photograph of Mala Silberberg at age two and a half, 1942. Gift of Samuel Klapholz, Yaffa Eliach Collection, donated by the Center for Holocaust Studies.

Rose and Mala managed to evade a children's *aktion,* in which the Nazis swept into the ghetto, tearing children away from their families and rounding them up for transport to the death camps. Mr. Silberberg contacted Mrs. Stanislawa Chicha, a Lithuanian woman who lived nearby in Sosnowiec, and offered to pay her if she would hide his family. An arrangement was made, and the Silberbergs found a way out of the ghetto.

Mrs. Chicha had a chicken coop connected to the back of her house. Moses Silberberg made the chicken coop livable and built a tiny underground bunker beneath it, complete with a trapdoor covered with potatoes to camouflage it. Into this cramped coop moved Rose, Mala, their parents, and their uncle. It was dark all the time, and they had to remain utterly quiet. The creaking floor could betray their presence to the passing Germans, or to visiting townspeople who might turn them over to the Germans.

The ordeal was particularly hard for Mala who, at only two and a half, found it difficult to be silent, and eventually she was sent to live with a Catholic family. The only arrangement her parents could make was that in exchange for protecting her, the family would adopt her and raise her as a Catholic. This at least might save their daughter's life.

As the months wore on, the rest of the family, hiding in the chicken coop, was beginning to starve. Mrs. Chicha's rations were insufficient to feed them all. The adults returned to the ghetto, where at least they could eat the meager ration provided, but Rose remained in the chicken coop alone. Mrs. Chicha brought her food. However, she was isolated for long hours in the darkness, and she grew very frightened. She was, after all, only nine. She begged to see her parents in the ghetto, and was eventually allowed occasional visits.

One of these visits occurred in early August 1943, when the general liquidation of the ghetto at Srodula had begun. The Germans surrounded the ghetto and began to search the buildings. Rose and her aunt hid in a bunker in the ghetto with other people, but they were discovered. Aunt Sara bribed the Jewish policeman who was guarding them to let Rose escape. Rose managed on her own to find her way back to Mrs. Chicha's house. A few days later, a few family members and other Jews who had evaded the roundup arrived at Mrs. Chicha's. The chicken coop now had sixteen people in it. They managed to live there, hidden and undetected, for six more months. In January 1944, the family that had been hiding Mala brought her to the chicken coop, unwilling to hide her anymore because their neighbors suspected that she was Jewish.

In February 1944, however, the SS, in their attempt to eliminate every Jew from every hiding place in the Sosnowiec area, surrounded Mrs. Chicha's house. All were forced out of the chicken coop. The girls' uncle pushed Rose and Aunt Sara toward the bunker beneath the chicken coop. Rose was old enough to scramble back down through the trapdoor, but Mala was asleep on the floor. She was caught, along with family members and others hiding in the chicken coop. Mrs. Chicha was also arrested; the crime of hiding Jews often incurred capital punishment. All were deported to Auschwitz-Birkenau. Long into that night, Rose still could hear the strong, powerful voice of four-and-a-half-year-old Mala screaming as the Nazis dragged her away: "Where is my sister? Where is my Aunt Sara?" Woken up at midnight by SS men in full gear, Mala was without winter clothes: she was taken to prison in her pajamas. The sound of her sister's screams haunted Rose for years.

An uncle, who had escaped during the melee, returned to open the bunker's trapdoor. He quickly offered advice about where to obtain identity papers. Rose and her aunt were able to get false working papers and were sent to work in Germany. Assuming identities as Christians, they worked serving meals in a convent. Even here, the SS stopped them and accused them of being Jewish. An SS officer pointed a revolver at Rose's head. "If you tell me you're Jewish, I'll let you go," he said. But she refused to be tricked. Remembering some of the Catholic liturgy she'd heard when her nursemaid had taken her to church, Rose recited prayers in Latin sufficiently well to convince the SS that they were not Jewish.

Rose and her Aunt Sara were finally liberated in April 1945. Returning to Poland to search for surviving family members, they discovered that all those sent to Auschwitz had been killed. They located Mrs. Chicha—only she had survived the death camp.

After spending time in a Kraków orphanage (and barely escaping with her life in a pogrom), Rose Silberberg and her aunt escaped again and finally immigrated to the United States in 1951. For sheltering the Silberbergs and many others during the Holocaust, Mrs. Chicha was recognized as one of the "Righteous Among the Nations" by Israel's Yad Vashem Holocaust Memorial in Jerusalem.

Photograph of Rose Silberberg, 1944. Gift of Rose Skier, Yaffa Eliach Collection, donated by the Center for Holocaust Studies.

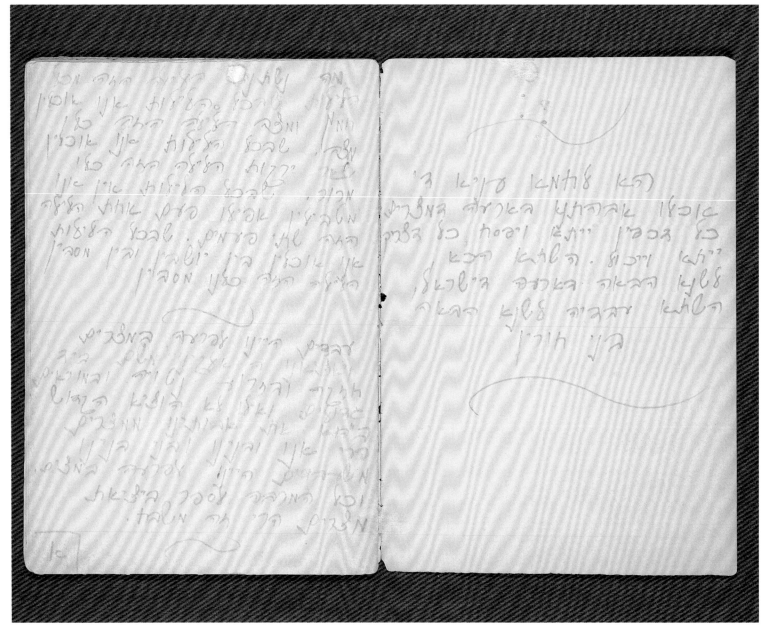

PASSOVER HAGGADAH

Handwritten Haggadah by Dina Kraus, Unterluss, Germany, 1944. Gift of Ludwig Ehrenreich, Zachary Ehrenreich, and Margaret E. Heching. Kraus wrote from memory, on illegally obtained paper, most of the Haggadah (Passover narration), and held a secret seder for the women in her camp barrack.

Dina Kraus Ehrenreich
The Secret Seder at Unterluss

My dear father!

This morning I received the most beautiful gift of my life. It was a Red Cross telegram that you are alive. Never in my life and never in the future will I ever be as happy. I just sent you a telegram. When did you return to Czechoslovakia? Where have you been? Are you healthy? Oh, Father . . .

I am writing you, my dear father, from my new position here. . . . I have twenty-nine nice children, mostly from Poland, ages eight to eighteen years. In the morning I am busy cleaning up, in the afternoon I teach again, Hebrew, Jewish history, and Swedish, the little I know, which is minimal.

Photograph of Dina Kraus in Czechoslovakia, circa 1946. Gift of Ludwig Ehrenreich, Zachary Ehrenreich, and Margaret E. Heching.

Dina Kraus wrote this letter to her father from the sanitarium in Sweden where she was recovering, only four months after her own liberation, near death, from Bergen-Belsen Concentration Camp in northern Germany. It expresses not only a delirious joy in finding a parent alive after the nightmare of the Holocaust, but also the pleasure and pride of returning to her profession as a teacher. The dedication to Jewish learning and practice, and the desire to share and transmit it even under the brutal conditions that prevailed during the Holocaust, may well have been what helped Dina Kraus—and many other religious Jews—remain alive through their ordeal.

Born in 1920 in Ungvar, a city in the Carpathian Mountains in what was then Czechoslovakia, Dina grew up in a strictly Orthodox family, excelled in her Jewish studies, and graduated from the Beth Jacob Hebrew Seminary, where she trained to be a teacher. She taught at Jewish schools, tutored privately, and then, as restrictions on Jewish activity increased, she returned home from Budapest to be with her family.

Following the Nazi occupation of Hungary in March 1944, all the Jews of Ung-

Photograph of Dina Kraus, possibly in a Purim outfit. Uzghorod, Czechoslovakia, circa 1928. Gift of Ludwig Ehrenreich, Zachary Ehrenreich, and Margaret E. Heching.

var were ordered in April to leave their homes. They were forced into a brick factory, used by the Nazis as a ghetto area. From here, when the deportations began, Kraus's family was broken up, and she was transported to Auschwitz-Birkenau in May. After several weeks, miraculously, she was able to discover and even communicate with her younger brother, Jidu, who had survived in the children's block in Camp D of the Auschwitz-Birkenau complex.

> Facing us came a group of small children carrying bricks. Among them was also my little brother in striped camp uniform . . . . We could see each other daily, throw letters to each other, and console and give hope to each other. He was so serious, sometimes I could not believe that he was my younger brother, who not long ago was the little, immature Jidu.

In September 1944, with the Germans relying more than ever on slave labor provided by the camp inmates, Dina Kraus was sent to a labor camp, Unterluss, near Hannover, in northern Germany.

Because of her fluency in German, she was assigned to be the clerk in the barrack and the distributor of the daily ration of soup. One day, as Passover, the Jewish festival of freedom, approached, a group of girls in the barrack asked her if she would conduct a secret seder.

A seder, the central observance of Passover, features the recitation of the Haggadah, the story of the Exodus from Egypt, told in Hebrew texts along with commentaries and songs. Dina Kraus set about organizing the telling of the Passover story in the barrack. Like any good teacher, she prepared. She drew on her memories of all the seders she had attended and taught about, and she summoned up the texts and the liturgy from her memory.

Then, with a pencil, she wrote down extensive sections of the Haggadah of Passover: *Hashatah avdei, l'shanah habah benai chorin*—"This year we are slaves, but next year we will be free."

It is hard to imagine the spiritual impact such words celebrating the promise of Jewish freedom had on the girls and young women in Dina Kraus's barrack. Urgently hushed, hummed, and whispered under the noses of the camp guards, who would have punished them severely for this infraction, these words were likely also being uttered in similar secret seders throughout the camp network of the Nazi forced labor and killing centers in occupied Europe.

Kraus survived and was liberated by British troops at Bergen-Belsen, where she had been transferred after Unterluss. After liberation, she thought again and often about Jewish learning. For it now began to re-center her life:

> In Bergen-Belsen I was deadly sick with typhus. . . . Only when the British left did I really know that I am alone. . . . Yet I was in a hospital in Malmoe [Sweden] for three weeks, it was in a school. . . . Slowly I found in myself a wish to return to real life, and when I heard that they were looking for a teacher for the refugee children coming to Sweden, I signed up. . . . I am writing you now, dear father, from my new position.

Dina Kraus's brother, Jidu, and her mother both were murdered at Auschwitz-Birkenau. She and her father immigrated to the United States in 1946. Her handwritten Haggadah is witness to the power of spiritual resistance in the shadow of death.

Dina Kraus Ehrenreich

Cover of Passover Haggadah, handwritten by Dina Kraus, Unterluss, Germany, 1944. Gift of Ludwig Ehrenreich, Zachary Ehrenreich, and Margaret E. Heching.

Photograph of Dina Kraus, standing second from right, with fellow students at the Beth Jacob Hebrew Seminary. Cernauti, Romania, circa 1934–1936. Gift of Ludwig Ehrenreich, Zachary Ehrenreich, and Margaret E. Heching.

BIRTHDAY GIFT

Heart-shaped clover given as a gift to Elizabeth Kroó. Lippstadt, Germany, March 16, 1945. Gift of Elizabeth Kroó Teitelbaum. The clover includes the initial "B" for "Bozsi," Kroó's nickname. The gift was made by her friends at a forced labor camp.

Elizabeth Kroó Teitelbaum

"If one girl turned, we all turned"

O ne day I was selected among others," recalled Elizabeth Kroó from her months in the women's barracks at Auschwitz-Birkenau in 1944, "but instead of being taken to the crematoria, we were stripped. Then they searched us everywhere—the mouth, ears, and vagina. At first we thought they were looking for gold and jewels." They were mistaken.

At Auschwitz-Birkenau and the other Nazi killing centers, elderly, middle-aged, and pregnant women, as well as mothers with children in tow, almost never survived and were gassed usually upon arrival. However, the young women who, like Elizabeth Kroó, survived the repeated selections, faced continuing and particular sexual risks, degradations, and assaults.

In addition to being forced to relinquish all their clothes and to wear ugly camp-issue rags, every emblem, token, and trace of the prisoners' femaleness was removed. Their hair was completely shaved, often including pubic hair. Their ration of thin soup led to malnutrition and extreme stress, which frequently resulted in interruption or stoppage of the menstrual cycle. This often led to the growth of facial hair and other conditions that undermined sexual identity.

It was perhaps to counter such deliberate humiliations that many women in the concentration camps bonded with each other and became as close as sisters, often replacing real-life sisters who had so recently gone to their deaths in the gas chambers.

In the barracks, they gave each other presents and marked birthdays with cards, gifts, and other remembrances that reinforced values such as friendship, affection, humor, hope, and compassion. In the face of persistent and desperate hunger, sickness, and disease unrelieved by medicine or even the means for basic hygiene, and despite the omnipresence of death, such gestures of friendship were an often crucial element in women's survival.

Birthday gifts for Elizabeth Kroó with "Keep Clean" in Hungarian. Lippstadt, Germany, March 16, 1945. Gift of Elizabeth Kroó Teitelbaum.

Elizabeth Kroó's early life in her hometown of Munkacs, in what was then Czechoslovakia, had, in many ways, prepared her to be a helper of others and, in turn, to receive their appreciation and love. Spurned and rejected by her stepmother, Elizabeth had been sent away at age fourteen to a girls' school and eventually went to live with her sister, Gabi, in Užhorod. In November 1938, Hungary annexed Munkacs and nearby towns such as Užhorod. When Elizabeth Kroó's brother-in-law was drafted into a Hungarian forced labor battalion, her sister had to maintain the family's small furniture business on her own.

Elizabeth was left in charge of the entire household, including three young nieces, Eva, Zsuzsi, and Lyvia. As the Hungarian Fascists implemented curfews and other severe restrictions, including allowing only an hour a day to shop, life became difficult, deeply frightening, and, at times, close to intolerable for Jews. Yet it got even worse in March 1944 when Germany occupied Hungary, and especially in April 1944 when the Jews were forced into ghettos.

Conditions were appalling, and typhus broke out. After a month, the Jews were marched through the streets toward the railroad tracks. Munkacs's non-Jewish citizens lined the streets, some sympathetic but others unabashedly proclaiming how happy they were to see the expulsion of the Jews. Kroó tried to camouflage her anguish. After all, she and her sister had three small children to look after. As young as they themselves were, they tried to reassure the children and struggled not to look riven with fear.

They marched on through the crowd, by turns silent, by turns jeering. Each of the little girls had a knapsack. Six-year-old Eva stopped to adjust a strap to keep her bag from slipping. One of the Arrow Cross (Hungarian Fascist) men rushed up and struck her hard on the shoulder with the butt of his rifle. All kept walking and boarded the cattle cars, with no idea of their destination as the door was bolted shut. Shortly after, a mother reached up and out the tiny window with a small cup to catch some rainwater for her thirsty child. Spotting the mother's hand, the German guard moved into position and shot the woman in the face. After that, the car erupted with wailing.

The Nazi strategy of terror and deception was such that Elizabeth Kroó and the others packed into the freight cars did not know they were leaving a transit point bound not for work in camps "in the east," but for the killing center at Auschwitz-Birkenau.

Birthday card with a humorous drawing and description of Elizabeth Kroó, cloth cover, embroidered on front, in Hungarian. Lippstadt, Germany, March 16, 1945. Gift of Elizabeth Kroó Teitelbaum.

Days later, when they emerged onto the platforms from the trains at Birkenau, they faced the first selection. Kroó was carrying her nine-month-old niece, Lyvia, while Gabi clutched the hands of the two other little girls. Suddenly, someone reached over and tore Lyvia from Elizabeth's arms. Elizabeth screamed, "She is my baby. We are together." But she was not believed. Lyvia was thrust into Gabi's arms, and then Elizabeth was separated from them and sent off in a different direction. She wondered how her sister was going to manage without her. Elizabeth worried about the bruise on Eva's shoulder until she learned—and it did not take long—that her sister and the girls were doomed to be gassed to death and then burned in the crematoriums.

Stripped and told to stand in the cold night air, Elizabeth Kroó and the other young women prisoners, not knowing what terror would befall them the next instant, took the only measures they could to give themselves comfort. With bodies freezing and teeth chattering, they moved together in bunches, their naked bodies touching to provide warmth.

In the barracks that first night—processed and shaved, and wearing the thin camp rags—they slept on the bare wood bunks. "We snuggled up to each other, one crotch in the other to keep each other's bodies from freezing. If one girl turned, we all turned."

Twice a day they lined up to be counted, at dawn and at twilight—always in the freezing weather. There were no showers and no soap. The sense of self, first as a woman and then as a human being, was assaulted. The hunger was constant, people grew weaker and sicker, and the selections continued.

Periodically they had to undress and line up completely naked in front of Josef Mengele, the chief doctor at Auschwitz, and others of the SS. They had to raise their arms high for bodily examination. Sisters, friends, and relatives clung together for support. The SS sent some to the gas chambers, leaving others alive—temporarily—to suffer particular grief.

Yet friendship and caring persisted. In the absence of soap, some of the women, desperate to wash and clean, used the white disinfectant that was used to spray in the toilet holes. As a result, many developed serious rashes and painful ulcers. Kroó's good friend Lola Katz, from Užhorod, died of her infections. Kroó nursed her and others as best she could.

Surviving more selections for the gas chambers, Elizabeth Kroó was sent, with a group of other young women, to Ravensbrueck and then to Lippstadt, in Germany. There they were housed in a camp near factories that manufactured airplane parts for the German air force. Her friends worked in the factory, and her assignment was to clean their barracks. The women were working with small, sharp instruments and were constantly cutting themselves, leaving many pus-filled suppurating wounds on their fingers. With no medicines or bandages, the wounds on some of the women's hands grew painful and dangerous. Kroó urged them to use their own urine as a disinfectant on their own infected fingers, and the suggestion worked.

As if responding to her caring spirit, Elizabeth Kroó's friends celebrated her birthday, which occurred during this period. Her friends somehow made her presents—humorous cards, a dustpan created out of stolen bits of scrap metal, and a pretty clover card. The gifts were made and given even though the Nazis considered stealing scraps to be sabotage, an act that would incur the death penalty.

In April 1945, when the factory was bombed by the Allies, and the Nazis knew the end was near, they assembled the surviving women workers into a long column and marched them out of Lippstadt, away from the advancing Soviet and American armies. Although conditions at Lippstadt were an improvement over what they had experienced at Auschwitz, the women were extraordinarily weak. Walking five, ten, twenty miles a day, these marches—death marches—were sustained at a deliberately killing pace. Anyone who dropped out or could not keep up was shot on the spot. The marchers lost all sense of time and geography.

Having survived countless selections and acts of terror, and now on the verge of rescue, the women felt themselves being pushed into a new torment. These death marches were instituted throughout the Nazi camp system in the waning days of the war and left numerous dead from exhaustion or execution by the roadside. To keep this from happening, Kroó and the other women, tired and sleepy beyond their own control, devised a system whereby they periodically exchanged places: one out of five—the person in the middle—could catch a few moments of sleep even while walking because the person in the middle would be dragged along by the others and not fall down and be shot. Exchanging places in this manner increased all their chances for survival.

The Allies grew closer, and the Nazi soldiers disappeared. Elizabeth and a friend escaped to the forest, but they were far from elated. They were lost, desperately hungry, and disoriented, although they were helped by a farmer, who let them sleep in his fields and barns. And yet they had to face a new fear: the farmer told them that the liberating Russians, who were all around them, were also on a raping rampage. Kroó hid in the house of the sympathetic farmer whenever the Russians approached. If they entered the house, she hid in the toilet, standing on the seat to avoid detection.

In the spring of 1945, Elizabeth Kroó finally found her way back home, only to confirm that most of her family had been killed, including two aunts, whom the Arrow Cross had pushed off a bridge to drown in the Danube. The spacious family house in Munkács was being used as a Russian military headquarters and hospital. Her sister's beautifully furnished house in Užhorod, where Elizabeth had lived and where she had helped care for the little girls, had been completely stripped. Torn pages from the family's Hebrew library were strewn about the rooms.

Eventually, Elizabeth Kroó Teitelbaum recovered, married, and settled in Brooklyn, New York. Her birthday gifts from the concentration camps are witnesses to the remarkable power of friendship: "Some people who survived the hell of the Holocaust have dignity and serenity and even hope beyond the average. . . . The effect has given many a unique knowledge and keen appreciation for freedom and for life that others may not possess."

Elizabeth Kroó Teitelbaum

Photograph of Elizabeth Kroó with other children dressed up for Purim in a private school in Slovakia, March 16, 1938. Gift of Elizabeth Kroó Teitelbaum.

RING

Made by Meyer Wagshlag for Celia Zelazna, at the HASAG ammunition factory near a forced labor camp. Skarzysko, Poland, 1944. Gift of Celia Levinsky. This simple ring, marked with Zelazna's initials, was her first personal belonging since the war began.

Celia Zelazna Levinsky
Celia's Ring

It is seven-eighths of an inch in diameter, scuffed, bent, and made of a discarded piece of chrome that has no monetary or utilitarian value whatsoever.

This ring, with twenty-two-year-old Celia Zelazna's initials inscribed on it, was given to her in a simple yet profound gesture of friendship in Skarzysko-Kamienna, a German forced labor camp in western Poland, in 1944. Celia Zelazna and her family had already been heckled and then attacked by rock-throwing anti-Semites in her hometown of Biała Podlaska; then, the Zelazna family was driven out of town to the Mezrich Ghetto.

One night, her two brothers did not return to the ghetto from forced labor, and Zelazna feared they had been killed. Early the next morning, Shabbat, the first day of Sukkot in 1942, the Nazis banged on the door during a roundup of remaining Jews. Zelazna's father, sensing that the family would never return, poured a large bottle of ink all over the heirloom dowry linens in the family hope chest, so at least they could not be used by the Nazis. Soon afterward, the Nazis deported the rest of her family to the Mezrich Ghetto, where they remained for a year. Her father was forced to remain in Biała Podlaska with the other men to clean up the ghetto, where he was later killed.

From the Mezrich Ghetto, the remaining Zelazna family was transported to the Majdanek death camp, where, within hours, the Nazis gassed Celia's mother, brother, and sister. Celia herself was spared—always temporarily—to do danger-ous labor. In Skarzysko, where she was transferred from Majdanek, she worked polishing parts for shells and other German munitions for the HASAG ammu-nition factory there. Zelazna was fortunately not in Skarzysko's Camp C, where underwater mines were manufactured. For this work, the forced laborers were required to handle dangerous acids. In Camp C, Zelazna's remaining younger brother was killed. It was no wonder that before the end of the war, 70 percent of the approximately twenty-eight thousand Jews brought to Skarzysko died.

In this world of imminent death, what a moment of wonder it must have been for Celia Zelazna when her friend, Meyer Wagshlag, who worked in the factory's precious-metal workshop, presented her with the ring.

A jeweler by trade, he had fashioned it from a scrap of chrome recovered from the factory floor and polished it to look like silver. Inscribing Zelazna's initials on it, along with the name of the factory and the year, Wagshlag imbued the ring with a power to do far more than memorialize the moment. For Zelazna, who had been stripped of home and family—every shred of what belonged to her emotionally and physically—the gift of the ring was a restoration of her sense of self and of humanity.

Yet Zelazna's ordeal was by no means over. As the Soviet army approached, the Nazis assembled the slave laborers for transportation to another camp in Germany. While she waited for the train to arrive, she noticed the SS guards were not about. After a moment of disbelief and bewilderment, it soon became clear that they had fled. After wandering for days and foraging for food, she and a group of

Photograph of Celia Zelazna.
Biała Podlaska, Poland, 1936.
Collection of Celia Levinsky.

other freed women found their way to Lodz, which had become the central gathering place for liberated Jews. Here, her first plan was to make her way back home to Biała Podlaska. She hesitated, however, when she heard that a Jewish woman had been murdered there when she returned to claim what was left of her house and possessions.

With that option no longer available and so many family members dead, Zelazna decided to leave Europe as soon as possible and to make contact with the only family she had in America, an aunt in New York City. To prepare for immigration, Zelazna made her way into the American zone of occupation to various Displaced Persons camps—Salzburg, Foehrewald, and, finally, Landsberg.

Here she met Abram Levinsky, who would eventually become her husband. In the Landsberg Displaced Persons Camp, Celia also re-met Meyer Wagshlag, originally from the same Polish town as her new husband. The friends continued to stay in touch in America through the Dzialoszyce *landsmanshaft,* an organization for natives of that small town near Kraków. After 1949, the Levinskys lived in New York and raised two daughters. Celia Zelazna and Abram Levinsky each were the sole surviving members of their families.

LODZ GHETTO WORK CARD

Work card issued to Juda Putersznyt. Lodz Ghetto, Poland, 1943. Gift of Elizabeth, Gail, and Sandy Peters. This work card identifies Juda Putersznyt as a carpentry instructor at the "small furniture factory" in the Lodz Ghetto. He and his wife, Rywka, were left behind to clean up the ghetto after it was liquidated. They were liberated by the Soviets.

Jerry and Regina Peters
A Story from the Lodz Ghetto

There were elegant four-tiered candlesticks on the table in front of them in January 1944 in the Lodz Ghetto. Friends and relatives gathered. The men wore hats, the women hats or scarves, and there were even smiles on the guests' faces. Of course, on such an occasion, everyone seemed a little stiff and nervous. For a wonderful ceremony—the marriage of Juda Putersznyt and Rywka Cala—was about to take place.

Despite accelerating brutality all around the incarcerated Jewish population, such assertions of human dignity, hope, and meaning through ritual and celebration were a form of resistance and a key to survival in the Lodz Ghetto and elsewhere during the Holocaust. Chaim Rumkowski, the head of the Jewish council, gave Putersznyt a ring so Juda could place it on the hand of Rywka, his bride.

In March 1939, Juda Putersznyt had been a young soldier in the Polish army. When his unit was captured by the Germans, he was imprisoned and spent some time in a prisoner-of-war camp. Because he was a Jew, he was stripped of his military status, uniform, and papers, and given a pass to return to Lodz, where he had been born.

When he returned, in April 1940, he discovered that the Germans had appropriated the family's venetian-blind factories. They had herded all the family members they could find, as with all Lodz's Jews, into the ghetto, which was set up in a slum quarter of the city. Here, approximately one hundred sixty-four thousand people were crammed, increasing the density of the zone seven-fold, in flimsy wooden houses with virtually no running water or sewers.

The Nazis immediately expropriated all Jewish property and factories, including the ones owned by the Putersznyt family. The factories were refitted to serve the German army and civilian population.

Photograph of a group wedding, including Juda Putersznyt and Rywka Cala. Lodz Ghetto, Poland, January 1944. Chaim Rumkowski is seated at the table. Gift of Elizabeth, Gail, and Sandy Peters.

Photograph of the interior of a workshop in the Lodz Ghetto, Poland. Gift of Elizabeth, Gail, and Sandy Peters.

The Jewish Council, or Judenrat, set up by the Nazis to coordinate internal ghetto affairs and the production of useful goods, organized one of the Putersznyt family's factories to produce wooden beds and toys for German children. With his knowledge of machinery and woodworking—having learned the business from his father, Israel—Juda Putersznyt became foreman of the factory. It was one of ninety-six factories employing tens of thousands of skilled, Jewish forced labor. The Jewish population's productivity was the primary reason the Nazis kept the ghetto population alive in Lodz after all the other ghettos in Poland had been destroyed. The leadership of the Judenrat, headed by Chaim Rumkowski, felt the only hope of saving some remnant of Jews from destruction was to keep the entire ghetto functioning as productively as possible.

For five years, Putersznyt worked in the factory, ten-hour days, with starvation rations that grew more meager as the war went on. The Nazis periodically entered the ghetto and removed the children, the elderly, the weak, and the many who had grown sick from malnutrition and the increasingly appalling conditions.

More than 20 percent of the population died in the ghetto from starvation, cold, and disease. Periodic deportations to Chelmno and other death camps also depleted the population. Because the ghetto was isolated not only from the world but also from other ghettos and even the Polish underground, the deported Jews did not have a clear idea of where they were being taken. Shortly after arrival at Chelmno, forty-seven miles west of Lodz, they were told they were being prepared to work in Germany, but they were to be gassed to death in specially equipped vans.

In spring 1944, the Soviet army reached the Vistula River, about seventy miles from Lodz. The Germans determined to eliminate all the Jews who remained alive in Lodz—approximately seventy thousand people. Among these were the most valued and skilled workers, such as Juda Putersznyt; his father, Israel; brother, Berek; and other workers whom they had managed to train. Included in this group was Rywka Cala, who had earlier come to work in the same factory.

By the fall of 1944, when the Russians began their final advance toward Lodz, almost all of the Jews who had been alive in the spring had already been transported to Auschwitz-Birkenau, where many were killed. Juda and Rywka Putersznyt were among a detachment of some eight hundred Jews whom the Nazis planned to murder last. They were left behind to pack the belongings of the deported Jews. As the Soviet guns were heard in the distance, an average of forty to sixty freight cars a day left the Lodz Ghetto, loaded with furniture and other personal possessions of every kind—all the Jewish community's property and all usable factory machines.

The ghetto's few remaining survivors now desperately hid from the Nazis. Even with the Soviets only a few kilometers away, the Nazis still went methodically from house to house through the ghetto to uncover the last survivors from their bunkers and hideouts in order to shoot them on the spot.

Rywka, Juda, and Israel Putersznyt, together with twenty-one others, discovered a large hidden closet within a closet, prepared and abandoned by another group of Jews. After three days without moving, they heard a family friend, who had been hiding in another bunker, shout, "Putersznyt, we are free. The Russians are here!"

On January 19, 1945, the three Putersznyts returned to their home and factory. Here, no longer pursued and hunted, they were eventually able to reestablish their lives. By the end of the 1950s, Israel Putersznyt had immigrated to Israel, while Juda and Rywka immigrated with their children to Canada and then to the United States. Because that first night of liberation was also a Friday night, Juda and Rywka Putersznyt lit candles and said the traditional blessings to welcome the Sabbath bride and to celebrate their freedom.

Birthday card for Juda Putersznyt, in Polish. Lodz Ghetto, Poland, May 10, 1944. Gift of Elizabeth, Gail, and Sandy Peters. This drawing was given to Putersznyt by his grateful students in a factory in the Lodz Ghetto, where they learned woodworking by making toys for German children.

TEFILLIN

Mismatched tefillin (worn by religiously observant men during weekly morning prayer), one of which was obtained by Shmuel Stern in exchange for a sweater. Buchenwald Concentration Camp, Germany, January 1945. Gift of Stanley Stern. In the camp, a sweater was precious; to Stern, the tefillin were even more so.

Stanley Stern
Tefillin

Shmuel Stern looked out from one of the prisoner kitchens at Buchenwald Concentration Camp. He had volunteered to work here in the hope of finding an extra potato peel to eat. What now drew him outside was an unaccustomed smell and sight—a plume of black smoke rising. This was unusual. For Buchenwald was not an extermination camp designed to gas and burn people, but rather a concentration camp, where one was weakened by work in the quarries or in the armaments factories in Buchenwald's 130 satellite camps and extension units.

Stern was naturally curious about the smoke. He went out the door, into the frigid winter air. What he saw filled him with great emotion: a large burning pile of Hebrew prayer books, prayer shawls, and black felt bags to carry religious articles. There were also scores of tefillin, sets of two small leather boxes containing within them tiny parchment scrolls on which were written selected texts from the Bible. When prisoners arrived at Buchenwald, one of the first acts of dehumanization inflicted on them was the order to turn over all personal possessions, including, of course, religious articles. On his arrival, Stern also had to relinquish his tefillin, which were now burning, he assumed, somewhere deep in the smoky fire.

Stern stepped back and noticed how the tangles of long leather straps that stretched out from the tefillin burned brightly. Religious Jews at morning prayers use the straps to bind the tefillin, one around the arm near the heart, the other around the forehead.

At the edge of the fire he now noticed one tefillin box, a half of a set of tefillin, that had not yet been consumed. He looked around to be certain that *kapos,* the prisoner trusties who enforced camp rules, were not nearby. Then he approached the fire's edge, bent down, rescued the tefillin, and hid it.

That night, he concealed it under his mattress, and he determined to put on the

Photograph of Shmuel Stern in Svalava, Czechoslovakia, September 7, 1939. Collection of Stanley Stern.

tefillin to pray in the morning. And yet, there was a serious problem, which now arose: How could he put on just one tefillin? Would it be permitted? The biblical commandment, from which the practice derived, stated clearly: "Bind them as a sign on your hand, and let them serve as a symbol on your forehead." In Buchenwald Concentration Camp, at the end of December 1944, how could he, prisoner number 27613, scrounging, like all the others, for food to stay alive, how could he find the second tefillin?

Wearing tefillin, as well as all other aspects of Jewish religious observance, had been intensely important to Shmuel Stern as a boy and young man growing up with four sisters and three brothers in the small town of Nelipeno, in what was then Czechoslovakia. He had gone to heder, Jewish religious school, every morning from six to eight before he went to public school. After regular school concluded, he returned to heder to pray the evening service and to study there from six to seven at night. Stern had also gone on to study at the Hebrew Gymnasium, in Munkacs, where even the general subjects were taught in Hebrew in order to prepare students for aliyah, immigration to Palestine. He couldn't decide if aliyah was for him. So many of the town's young people had already gone off in far different directions—to Russia to escape the encroaching Germans or to America, where some had found brides and bridegrooms. However, Shmuel Stern's difficult decision was rendered moot when the war came to Nelipeno.

As he lay on his thin mattress that night in Buchenwald, Stern could remember the sights and smells of his religious home life and his town: the challah, the braided egg-bread that his mother prepared every Sabbath; the *cholent,* the traditional bean-and-potato Sabbath food she always prepared and kept warm in the stove in their small grocery store. He also remembered his hometown synagogue on Yom Kippur, filled with fervent confessions and prayers, and the building's aisles lined with memorial candles, each standing tall inside a pumpkin half-filled with sand so it would not tip over.

Stern was eighteen years old, and the notice drafting him into a Hungarian forced labor unit came on the last day of Passover, 1943. He managed to convince the Hungarian authorities that he was a professional electrician, and he worked as such in several factories outside of Budapest until October 1944. The Germans began to apply increasing pressure to implement the "final solution" to Hungarian Jews, including those, like Shmuel Stern, in the forced labor units.

Stern escaped with a friend and made his way to Budapest. They had heard that

Raoul Wallenberg and other diplomats of neutral countries were distributing documents there that might protect them from arrest and deportation.

Although Stern did not secure protective papers, he did locate a safe house operated by Swedish officials—nominally neutral territory—and remained there for two precious months of refuge. Then, Hungarian Fascists, working on behalf of the Nazis and using the ruse that they were recruiting volunteers for work, broke in and arrested the refugees. Stern was packed, along with ninety-four others, into a locked railroad car. Eighteen excruciating days later, he arrived at Buchenwald.

Now, the day after he had found the single tefillin, Shmuel Stern had little or no expectation of finding a second tefillin box. He was marched to the munitions factory in nearby Magdeburg, one of the subcamps of Buchenwald, where he worked at electrical tasks in the making of ammunition. If he and the other workers could get away with sabotaging some of the military products, they would do so.

At the end of the shift, when they were marched back to camp, Stern saw a second remarkable sight: another prisoner holding in his hand an object that looked curiously like a tefillin piece. The additional miracle was that it did not duplicate what he had, but would now make a complete set—one box for the heart and now one for the head. Since the prisoner was a Gypsy—and not Jewish—Stern was able to trade a sweater for the second tefillin box.

The next morning, and each morning thereafter, first Stern and then the other Jewish prisoners who chose to borrow them, put on the tefillin and said their morning prayers, joyfully fulfilling, for the first time in months, these important religious commandments.

Stern kept the tefillin always with him when he was transferred to a factory in Polta, another satellite of Buchenwald. In the waning days of the war, Stern and his friends escaped from the factory and hid in a cellar for seven days. They emerged in April 1945 as the liberating American armies approached.

From Belgium, where his health was restored, to Brooklyn, where he arrived in 1946 to meet the only members of his family to survive (a brother and a sister who had emigrated in the 1930s), and through the years of marriage and raising a family in New York, the tefillin stayed with him. He deliberately allowed them to remain scuffed and refrained from repairing the tefillin, to preserve them exactly as he had found them at Buchenwald. Shmuel, now Stanley, Stern used them for many years as the centerpiece of a presentation he made to schoolchildren in the New York City area.

Stanley Stern

Portrait of Shmuel Stern in Horsfalva, Czechoslovakia, April 3, 1943. Collection of Stanley Stern.

FALSE IDENTITY CARD

False ID card used by Cornelia Braun, in the name of Kornelia Brasinova. Bratislava, Slovakia, June 20, 1944. Gift of John Balan. Alexander Braun and Karel Palasthy prepared false papers for the Braun family, who were in hiding, using potatoes sliced in half to transfer ink stamps onto the documents.

John Balan
Family in Hiding

In January 1945, two men were walking single file down a freezing and dark street in Bratislava, Slovakia, a puppet ally of Nazi Germany since 1939. There were perhaps a dozen paces between them, and the man in the lead, Karel Palasthy, was carrying a hand-powered flashlight. If he flashed the color green, the man behind, Alexander Braun, continued to proceed. If, however, Palasthy noticed a patrol of German soldiers or Slovak collaborators, he flashed red, and Braun dashed off the street. He hid until the green flashing again indicated the danger had passed.

Alexander Braun was making his nightly visit to his ten-year-old son, Jan, who was hiding—like himself but in a different location—from the rapidly accelerating Nazi roundups. The danger was great, but Braun was determined to see his son.

It had not always been this way.

In 1934, Jan was born the only child of Alexander and Cornelia Braun into an upper-middle-class family in Bratislava, then the capital of the province of Slovakia in the Czechoslovak republic. With a father who had been a dashing officer in the Austro-Hungarian army in World War I and a mother who was converted to Christianity, Jan led a highly assimilated life. Father and son themselves converted to Christianity in Bratislava's Hungarian Reform Protestant Church in 1938. This was a step that they hoped might provide them some protection from the harassment already seen in Germany and the severe anti-Jewish riots then expected and being orchestrated by the Hlinka Guard, an ultranationalist Slovak pro-Nazi militia.

However, as long as the Germans did not actually occupy Slovakia, life was tolerable for the Brauns. Jan's family operated a gourmet grocery store, their circle included many Christians, and they were exempted from wearing the yellow star and from the deportations being supervised by the Nazi expert on "the Jewish problem," Adolf Eichmann.

In 1942, as the Slovaks maneuvered and competed with the Nazis to exploit Jewish labor and to appropriate—"Aryanize"—Jewish property, the Brauns still survived. Although the business was lost, the previous baptism, for a time, helped. Fifty-eight thousand Slovak Jews were deported to the east from March to October 1942—most to die in the death camps.

However, as the Germans now moved into Slovakia, Aryan papers no longer provided the *vynimka,* the protection or exemption from deportation, that had been keeping the family alive.

Alexander Braun's store had already been confiscated, and he had been forced into more meager employment, but the situation was getting even worse: a Slovak version of the Nuremberg Laws was now brutally enforced. The only hope was false identity and, eventually, hiding. Jan Braun, who was to become Viktor Bratkovic, Peter Dubravicky, Jan Abranic, and a variety of other names, was able to continue to avoid detection and even to attend elementary school.

Nora Palasthyova, a teacher in the school, became particularly fond of Jan and befriended his parents. In 1944, as a result of a major partisan uprising, the Germans occupied Slovakia in earnest, and all pretenses were off. The Palasthys had the Brauns sleep over many evenings because the Nazi roundups occurred in the very early morning hours. They were spared again.

However, on September 28, 1944, the Hlinka Guard came literally to their door: that night, as it turned out, was the *velka chytacka* (big roundup), of Bratislava Jews. Jan Braun later described what occurred: "At the Palasthys, we heard the noise of the roundup from within the apartment. It was a large building, with a number of staircases. We were on the very top floor to which one of these led. I believe the searchers stopped on the floor just below. 'Let's go,' they called out, 'there are no more Jews left here.' A miracle . . ."

In the following days, Jan was hidden in a large suitcase on top of a closet, and several times his father had to climb outside and hide in a window box. During the following nights, Karel Palasthy took the Brauns to a coal cellar in the basement. During the days, strict silence was enforced, as there was supposed to be no one in the apartment. The Nazis and their collaborators searched for the re-

Hand-powered flashlight used by Alexander Braun. Bratislava, Slovakia, 1944. Gift of John Balan. Alexander Braun used this flashlight in hiding in the coal cellar and to visit his son in a separate hiding place at night. Karel Palasthy used a similar flashlight that also had red and green lights to signal whether or not it was safe for Braun to proceed. The flashlight worked by pumping the lever.

maining Jews with a terrifying thoroughness. When someone who knew their hiding places was arrested in January, the family feared their own discovery was only a matter of time.

Using potatoes sliced in half to transfer ink stamps from real onto false documents, the Palasthys helped the Brauns establish new identities yet again (Jan Braun/Viktor Bratkovic was now Peter Dubravicky). They also helped them to find new—and now separate—hiding places. They moved from place to place only at night, with Jan's mother and father eventually having to escape by leaving Bratislava. Jan, however, remained hidden with several families and protected by the Palasthys, first in Bratislava and then in the countryside, where he survived until liberation.

Reunited with his family after the Soviet army passed through Slovakia, Jan Braun and his parents became the Balans, immigrated to the United States in 1948, and later established contact with surviving cousins, now in Israel. Many less fortunate members of the extended Braun family were gone. For risking their lives daily to save the Brauns and for shining a light of humanity—a red and green flashlight—during the darkness of the Holocaust, Karel and Nora Palasthy have been formally designated "Righteous Among the Nations" by Israel's Yad Vashem Holocaust Memorial in Jerusalem.

John Balan

Photograph taken in April 1944 of Jan Braun at age ten in Bratislava, Slovakia. Gift of John Balan.

ARMY INSIGNIA

Worn by Chanan Arnold Levinsky, issued by the British army in Palestine, 1941. Gift of Arnold H. Levinsky. Levinsky, born in Germany, entered Palestine illegally in 1939. He joined the British army in 1941 and served with the Jewish Brigade.

Arnold Levinsky
A Soldier of the Jewish Brigade

In 1941, before he proudly sewed onto his sleeve the insignia of the Jewish Brigade of the British army, with the Hebrew acronym for Jewish fighting forces, Chanan Arnold Levinsky had been a *halutz,* a pioneer in Palestine. But the story begins earlier, in a Europe lurching toward war.

In 1935, sixteen-year-old Hans Arnold Levinsky was abruptly called out of his classroom and into the office of the director of his high school in Bad Polzin, Germany. Arnold was a good student; he had done nothing wrong, and he was deeply disturbed to hear the news presented to him. He was informed that his fellow students refused to continue learning as long as there were Jews in the classroom. He was ordered to leave immediately.

This event shocked Levinsky and drove him even closer into his family's longstanding involvement in local Zionist youth movements. Arnold's older brother was already participating in He-Halutz, a Zionist youth movement founded in Germany in 1918. Their aim was to train members to settle in Palestine. However, since the British, who controlled the country, were severely restricting immigration to Palestine, He-Halutz shifted the focus of its work from immigration to *hakhsharah,* preparation for eventual immigration through training in agricultural and vocational education.

Levinsky joined his brother on a *hakhsharah* farm in Grusen, Germany. However, in 1938, when it became increasingly difficult to operate in Nazi Germany, the movement went underground, and its members dispersed. Arnold went to a *hakhsharah* farm in Holland, not far from Amsterdam. Within a year, he received a telegram advising him to leave shortly for Palestine. The ship would be illegal, but war was looming, and settlement in Palestine was the ultimate goal of Levinsky's training.

Sports blouse worn by Mary Offentier, from the Bar Kochba sports club. Berlin, Germany, 1936–1938. Gift of Mary Levinsky. From 1936 to 1938, Mary Offentier was a member of a Zionist sports club named for the ancient Jewish hero Simon Bar Kochba. After Kristallnacht, when her parents illegally sent their daughters to Holland, Mary packed the sports blouse among her most loved belongings. Eventually, Mary was reunited with her parents, and they spent two years in hiding before they were liberated in Brussels in September 1944. There, Mary met and eventually married Chanan Arnold Levinsky of the Jewish Brigade.

Four weeks later, packed with one thousand five hundred people, the *Dora* departed Amsterdam. After a voyage of four weeks, she approached the coast of Palestine. It was hardly a coincidence that shortly before the ship's arrival the British coast guard facility had been bombed by the Haganah, the underground Jewish defense force. Under cover of night, Levinsky and the other *halutzim* swam ashore, and walked miles to a kibbutz, where they spent their first night in "Eretz Israel."

The next morning, Zionist dream met the tough reality of primitive living conditions and severe food shortages on the kibbutz where Levinsky began to work. Still, he was where he wanted to be, and war had broken out in Europe two weeks after his arrival. For the foreseeable future, there would be few new arrivals, so each *halutz* took on a heavy load of work responsibilities. Eventually, Levinsky moved to kibbutz Ashdot Ya'akov, where he learned the baker's trade.

Years earlier, in 1940, Chaim Weizmann, president of the World Zionist Organization, had attempted to create a Palestinian Jewish fighting force in the British army, but discussions went nowhere. During the course of the war, two developments occurred that led to the creation of a brigade group, formed of volunteers from Palestine within the British army. For one, the British military position in Egypt and the Middle East was deteriorating under attacks of German general Erwin Rommel. The British asked for Arab and Jewish volunteers for the British army. In August 1942, thousands of Palestinian Jews volunteered to join the Palestine Regiment, originally planned as a unit of three Jewish battalions and one of Arabs. Second, news of the murder of the Jews of Europe reached Palestine by November 1942.

As the extent and degree of Nazi atrocities became clearer, soldiers in the Jewish battalions, including Levinsky, demanded that a distinct Jewish fighting force be created. Jews had been agitating for a Jewish unit since the outbreak of the war. They now also put pressure on the British War Office to shift the force from the support duties they were performing in Palestine and Egypt to combat-related duties, so they could now more directly fight the Nazis. Many dreamed of also helping to rescue Jews in Europe.

In part because of the press of public opinion and also because it now seemed morally untenable to prevent Jewish soldiers from fighting the Nazis, one of the sections within the Palestine Regiment was finally transformed: by order of the British War Office, in September 1944, it became the Jewish brigade group. Its commander was Brigadier Ernst Benjamin, and the Zionist flag was officially approved as its standard.

Three infantry battalions of the Jewish Brigade were assembled in Egypt in early 1945, and Levinsky was with one in Alexandria, where he worked as a dispatch rider on a motorcycle. Then the brigade took part in the early stages of the final Allied offensive in Italy in April 1945. There, on the front line, the brigade was finally fighting the Nazis.

Soldiers like Levinsky were role models—even heroes—to many of the young Jewish men and women who had survived the concentration camps. He and other brigade members helped to smuggle some of them from the Displaced Persons camps in Italy into Palestine. Brigade members made special efforts to get into the liberated areas—often disobeying army orders—to help the survivors.

In Brussels to visit family after the war, Levinsky met his future wife, Mary Offentier, also originally from Germany. She had spent years in hiding in Holland and was liberated in Brussels in 1944. Levinsky was discharged from the British army and returned to Palestine, where he saw service in the Israeli War of Independence. The couple eventually immigrated to America in 1957.

Of the 5,000 soldiers who had served in the Jewish Brigade, Chanan Arnold Levinsky was one of 323 members to be decorated. The Jewish Brigade was the first and only Jewish unit to fight in World War II under its own flag, recognized as representing the Jewish people.

LIBERATION DRESS

Made by Frania Bratt in a satellite camp of the Dachau Concentration Camp. Germany, May 1945. Gift of Frania Bratt Blum. Frania Bratt used fabric supplied by the U.S. Army to make new dresses for herself and her sister, Helen, to replace their striped inmate uniforms. Other women also stitched new garments from the donated bolts of cloth—those able to sew helping those who did not know how or were too weak.

Frania Bratt Blum

The Liberation Dress

What goes through a young woman's mind when she sews her own dress? For twenty-seven-year-old Frania Bratt in early May 1945, in a satellite of Dachau Concentration Camp, near Munich, Germany, we may guess: a sense of freedom and a renewal of her life as a human being, a Jew, and a woman.

On April 29, the camp had finally been liberated by the Seventh Army of the United States Armed Forces. Like many of the 67,000 inmates packed into Dachau's barracks by hastily retreating Nazis in the last days of the war, Frania Bratt had survived several other camps. For more than sixteen months, she had worn only the standard inmate uniform, but now, slowly, her sense of individuality was beginning to return as she sat thinking about sewing a dress. She had before her bolts of cheerful blue-and-white-checked fabric that had been provided by the U.S. liberators.

A close friend of Frania's cut the cloth, and Frania began. She knew how to sew, and along with professional seamstresses who had survived, she helped others who were too dazed or weak to complete the project on their own. Such mutual support and acts of caring had, in no small measure, been responsible for the survival, both physical and emotional, of many of the women. When Bratt completed her dress, all the work done by hand, she sewed another one for her sister, Helen, who was too sick to make one herself. Imagine what the moment was like when the sisters first put them on together.

Frania Bratt fashioned the dress in the peasant style, which she had admired as a young girl growing up in southern Poland before the war. But there was much in Polish life—in particular the frequent outbreaks of anti-Semitic violence—that was far from admirable. Frania was born into

Wedding invitation hand printed by Boris (Borys) Blum for the celebration of his wedding with Frania Bratt. Landsberg Displaced Persons Camp, Germany, January 6, 1946. Gift of Frania Bratt Blum.

a large Orthodox family in a rural community, where her father owned a lumber-yard near the city of Czestochowa. In 1921, after he was murdered by an anti-Semite, the family's economic condition declined.

With their occupation in September 1939, the Nazis implemented a strategy of terror followed by public humiliation, isolation, and dehumanization. Massive restrictions were imposed on the Jews of Czestochowa and the neighboring towns. Then a ghetto was established. Sensing that worse was coming, some members of Bratt's family—including a brother, a sister, and a niece—went into hiding in 1940. They were soon found, taken to the nearby forest by the Nazis, and shot.

In September 1942, roundups and selections for transport from the ghetto began. Bratt remembers the precise morning hour—5:00 A.M.—when three of her sisters were seized. During this period, Frania's mother had a stroke, and Bratt tried desperately to stay close to her and nurse her. She and her mother were hiding in a bunker when her mother died. In 1943, the ghetto was liquidated, and Frania Bratt began her horrific odyssey through Bergen-Belsen and a network of Nazi camps that led her finally to Dachau.

But now, after liberation, she had the dress, and that was only the beginning of her new life. At the Landsberg Displaced Persons (DP) Camp she met Boris (Borys) Blum. Also a Holocaust survivor, he was now an officer with the United Nations Relief and Rehabilitation Administration (UNRRA). His job was to distribute supplies to the scores of thousands of displaced persons whose ranks were growing at Landsberg and the other camps. Many Jewish survivors had found, on returning to their homes in Eastern Europe, that anti-Semitism still remained strong. Many survivors felt they could not renew their life in their hometowns. At the DP camps, particularly those in the American occupation zone of Germany, there was at least hope of immigration to Palestine, the United States, or Canada.

Under Boris's supervision, Bratt worked as a member of the UNRRA team to help set up a kosher communal kitchen. She took particular pleasure in setting out clean napkins and silverware at each meal, so that diners might feel that they were eating, once again, like human beings.

She also happened to fall in love with Boris Blum. They had a small mar-

Photograph of Frania Bratt Blum holding her daughter, Towa, in the Landsberg Displaced Persons Camp. Germany, 1946. Gift of Frania Bratt Blum. Blum is wearing the dress she made in the liberated Dachau Concentration Camp.

Photograph of Boris Blum supervising food distribution in the Landsberg Displaced Persons Camp. Germany, circa 1947. Gift of Frania Bratt Blum.

riage ceremony in September 1945 and then a large celebration in January 1946. The invitation to their wedding states with proud irony not only their birthplaces but also one of the concentration camps they each had survived. When their daughter, Towa, was born, the Blums took many photographs with her and the many other new Jewish mothers and their babies born at Landsberg and the other DP camps.

In 1950, Frania Bratt Blum, Boris Blum, and Towa (later Toby) were able to immigrate to the United States. Settling in Brooklyn and raising her family, Bratt, over the years, often took her dress out of the closet and examined it and mended it. She wore her blue-and-white-checked dress to mark the anniversary of her liberation day and other happy occasions, such as her children's birthdays.

The liberation dress is regularly on display at the Museum, where it is featured in the exhibition on the aftermath of the Holocaust. It represents hope, signifying Frania Bratt's return to humanity and her longing for the future.

Photograph of Frania, Boris, and Towa Blum in the Landsberg Displaced Persons Camp. Germany, 1947. Gift of Frania Bratt Blum.

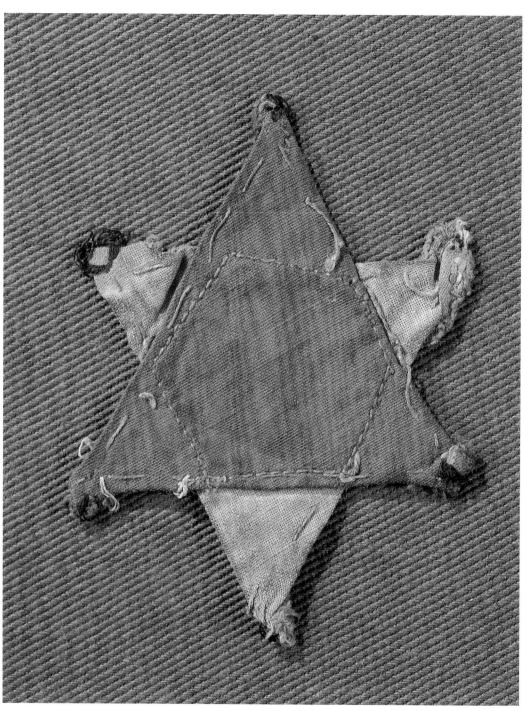

CLOTH STAR

Star given to Peretz Milbauer by a survivor. Waldenburg, Germany, 1945. Gift of Peretz and Blanche Milbauer. Peretz (Perry) Milbauer was a member of the 179th Engineers Combat Battalion stationed in Remse, Germany. He led a small delegation of American soldiers to take supplies to 2,200 Jews who had been on a death march and were currently staying in the town of Waldenburg. The star was probably made after the liberation.

Peretz (Perry) Milbauer

"I just had to write this letter in Yiddish"

I n the spring of 1945, units of the American, British, and Soviet armies were converging on Germany in the final phase of World War II. Whether as liberators of the concentration camps or in their encounters with groups and columns of disoriented, starving former prisoners along the road, Allied soldiers, even those accustomed to suffering and death on the battlefield, were very shaken by these initial contacts with Holocaust survivors.

Meeting the survivors and hearing them tell their stories for the first time had an especially profound effect on Jewish GIs. One such encounter occurred on April 15, 1945, near the town of Waldenburg, in Silesia. Master Sergeant Peretz (Perry) Milbauer of the 179th Engineers Combat Battalion of the American Third Army, which was encamped in Remse, Germany, was among the first soldiers in that area to come across survivors of a death march: a group of twenty-two hundred starving people whom the Nazi guards, in their attempt to escape before the Allied advance, had abandoned by the roadside.

Sergeant Milbauer's letter, written to his wife on the same day, captured the dazed astonishment, anxiety, and awe of those who seemed to be awakening from certain death to new life. It also pointed to the immense new challenges facing the victors: how to help the survivors restart their lives, how to punish the murderers, and how to make sense of the suffering. The world would struggle with these questions for decades to come.

> April 15, 1945
> Dear Blanche,
> I just had to write this letter in Yiddish. . . . Why Yiddish? It is because all my Jewishness has welled up in me, I feel myself completely a Jew. Also, since a Jewish historical situation is involved, I can only write in Yiddish.

Imagine! Midday today a Jewish GI came to me and said there were three Jews on the other side of the street. When I went over, before I could speak, one of the trio said in Yiddish, "He has a Jewish face." I answered in Yiddish whereupon the three wished me well and blessed me to the very skies. . . . Oh how happy they were!

I soon learned that located in a nearby town was a group of Jews taken from concentration camps, that the retreating Germans were driving in front of them. There were about two thousand Jewish women, mostly from Hungary, and two hundred men, chiefly from Poland. They had been in different concentration camps including Auschwitz-Birkenau.

They were force marched thirty kilometers in twelve hours without food and with only one thirty minute rest period. They were overjoyed when the column leader strayed and went twelve kilometers down a wrong road. At night he hid them in a wood. In the morning, American tanks came along, and they were suddenly "free." I use quotation marks because many told me later, "Yes, we are free but we can't quite comprehend what that means, we cannot understand freedom."

We loaded up the three men with food and soap and took a variety of supplies to the nearby town. There I greeted my fellow Jews with a hearty "Sholom Aleichem!" At first the Jews were skeptical. Very weakly they questioned, "Are you a Jew?" When I answered "Yes," they became joyful and poured out their hearts to me.

It is impossible to report everything. . . . the refugees described how pleased they were that the Americans were here. How did they put it? "Angels?" "The Messiah has already come." One individual added that we will have a new Passover, [celebrating] not deliverance from Egyptian slavery but escape from the clutches of the Nazis. Then they started to describe their tribulations and mistreatment by the Germans. I listened endlessly to stories. But all the experiences—children's heads smashed against walls, the crematoria, wanton killings, working twelve hours at night without sleeping during the day, being the only family survivor . . . Can anything be worse than what we already know?

How did one man put it earlier in the day? "In five years I had no one to cheer me up, with whom can I now share my joy? I have no one. I can't go home and tell my wife: 'Look, the Americans have given me food.' But I can't even share this happiness with anyone."

Questions were asked: "Did Americans know what was happening here?" "Did people believe it?" I answered, confirming that there were reports that many had believed from the start, but that everyone was now convinced of the atrocities. I felt that in reply there would be a protest that we in America knew but did nothing. No one registered that complaint. . . .

I also asked for the names of those who had families in other countries. I would see to it that the lists were printed in the Jewish newspapers. . . . One survivor asked me why I was so interested. I answered, "Because I am a Jew." His response was to give me an affectionate pat.

I am sorry that I am not a writer and am not able to give a better report. There is so much to describe. I am overwhelmed. . . .

Blanche Milbauer, who worked in New York at the YIVO Institute for Jewish Research, saw to it that these survivors' names, and those of their relatives in America and Palestine, were soon published. Calls immediately flooded into YIVO as American family members began to learn of the survival and liberation of their loved ones.

In Waldenburg, Sergeant Milbauer spoke to a U.S. Army lieutenant who then went to the mayor of the town and ordered him to provide the survivors with food. Within two days, all 2,200 death march survivors were also sleeping inside houses, for the first time in years, like people once again.

But the story does not end here. A month later, Sergeant Milbauer was at the concentration camp at Ebensee, Austria. From here, he wrote his wife:

> It is really impossible to describe the living. Some did not have a human expression at all. . . . American medics are caring for them. Two busloads were evacuated, and it was pitiful to see others trying to crawl on the roof of the ambulance—a mass of bones with a spark of life!

He closed his letter to his wife by reporting to her that for some of his fellow soldiers, it took actually seeing "live models to really convince them that what they heard was true. One told me as we were coming back, 'And I thought it was propaganda.' "

Peretz (Perry) Milbauer

Photographs of the Ebensee Concentration Camp in Austria, taken by Peretz Milbauer after liberation in May 1945. Gift of Peretz and Blanche Milbauer.

PHOTOGRAPH OF A HANUKKAH CELEBRATION

Vida Kaufman seated in the background. Bergen-Belsen Displaced Persons Camp, Germany, 1946–1948. Gift of Judith Naomi Fish. Vida Kaufman worked for the American Jewish Joint Distribution Committee (JDC) and was assigned to the Bergen-Belsen Displaced Persons Camp. This photograph was included in an album given to Kaufman in appreciation of her work. On the inside of the album is the inscription in Yiddish: "To remember the children of Bergen-Belsen, an expression of love for Vida Kaufman, Bergen-Belsen, January 21, 1948."

Vida Kaufman
"Where will we go?"

Vida Kaufman had followed the progress of World War II from afar—the safety of New York City. Yet as a Jew born into a religious family in Dukla, Poland, in 1902, she felt particularly connected to the plight of the Polish and Eastern European Jews who had survived the Holocaust and were now trying to rebuild their shattered lives. Most now looked to the Allies, and westward, for help.

On Victory in Europe, or VE, Day, May 8, 1945, there were one and a half to two million displaced persons (DPs) in Europe—many who could not be repatriated to their prewar homes because they feared retribution, economic deprivation, or continuing attempts at annihilation.

Of these DPs there were approximately two hundred thousand Jewish survivors of the forced labor and extermination camps, death marches, and partisan units, as well as those who had spent the war years in the Soviet Union or had survived in hiding. Those from Western European countries generally returned home. However, many of the Jewish survivors from Poland, Russia, and the central European countries believed that the lesson of the Holocaust was that Jews must take control of their own fate. Most of these survivors determined to start new lives in Palestine. Many sought to join their families in the United States.

By 1946, Vida Kaufman was an accomplished administrator in Jewish communal organizations. She applied to the American Jewish Joint Distribution Committee (known as "the Joint") to work in Europe with the Holocaust survivors. Along with large numbers of new Jewish refugees fleeing from the continuing anti-Semitism in their hometowns and villages in Eastern Europe, survivors were streaming into the DP camps, primarily in the British and American zones of occupation in Germany and camps in Austria and Italy.

Although at this time the camps were operated by the military, basic food and other services were supplied by recently established international organizations such as the United Nations Relief and Rehabilitation Administration (UNRRA) set up in 1943. Jewish agencies, such as the Joint, and Zionist emissaries from Palestine were also providing humanitarian aid in education, welfare, health, and immigration services for the survivors.

On July 15, 1946, Vida Kaufman arrived as a Joint welfare worker to the DP camps in the British-occupied zone of Germany. She served on a team sent by the Joint to improve conditions of the survivors at the main DP camp in the British zone at Bergen-Belsen. It was on the site of what had been the SS quarters for the concentration camp. Although the barbed wire and other signs of incarceration under the Nazis were gone, the needs of the survivors, many shattered physically and emotionally, were daunting. Sanatoriums and children's homes were set up; medical care and legal assistance were provided; and schools, yeshivas, and synagogues were established.

Survivors were also active in setting up their own political and social organizations as well as registries to reconnect with loved ones—and to find out what happened to them. Telegrams came and went, people desperately were trying to find husbands, wives, brothers, and sisters. Few old people and fewer children had survived the camps. Many of the survivors were eager to start families. There were marriages and a baby boom, and at Bergen-Belsen, Kaufman participated in celebrating the birth of the thousandth baby in the camp. All this also meant nurseries and kindergartens, which Vida Kaufman helped to supervise.

Photographs from an album given to Vida Kaufman by those she worked with at the Bergen-Belsen Displaced Persons Camp, Germany, 1946–1948. Gift of Judith and Naomi Fish. Wearing glasses and a big smile, Kaufman is seated (photo on left, center) at a children's party at the camp.

Photograph from an album given to Vida Kaufman from the illegal immigrants of the ship *Exodus 1947*. Gift of Judith Naomi Fish. The *Exodus 1947* reaching the port of Haifa. The ship's journey was timed to coincide with the visit of the United Nations Committee on Palestine so that the members of the committee might witness the restrictive British immigration policy.

The Joint was soon financing the greater part of the welfare, cultural, and educational activities in the camp.

As an administrator who spoke English, Yiddish, and Hebrew, Kaufman was invaluable, and she also brought great interpersonal skills to bear in the midst of a highly emotional and potentially chaotic situation. She worked with hundreds of individuals, and functioned as a liaison officer to many other organizations, Jewish and non-Jewish, that were providing services to the refugees. She participated in the establishment and development of a school system for the survivors, from nursery schools through high school.

The learning of modern Hebrew at Bergen-Belsen and the other DP camps—much of which Vida soon began to supervise as the director of education and chief welfare officer for the British zone—had far more than educational and cultural significance. To learn Hebrew, in the view of the Zionist organizations and youth groups active in the camp, was to prepare to live, ultimately, in the future Jewish state.

Kaufman arrived at Bergen-Belsen shortly after the visit there by David Ben-

Gurion, the leader of the Jewish community in British-occupied Palestine. With a quota of 1,500 legal immigrants a month strictly enforced, Ben-Gurion's visit galvanized the Zionist youth groups and survivor organizations in the DP camps. These organizations regarded the plight of the survivors and other displaced persons as an important means to focus the world's attention on the issue of Jewish self-determination. They joined with Jewish leaders in Palestine to promote a program of Aliyah Bet, or illegal immigration. Their aim was both to smuggle Jews to "Eretz Israel," or the Land of Israel, and also to force the political issue of the establishment of a Jewish state.

Six months after Vida Kaufman arrived in Germany, the ship that would come to be known as *Exodus 1947* was acquired by the leaders of Aliyah Bet. On July 11, 1947, at dawn, the ship, loaded with forty-five hundred refugees, many with whom Vida had previously worked in Bergen-Belsen, sailed from the French port of Sète for the shores of Palestine. The refugees vowed never to return to Europe, but British destroyers, with other intentions, accompanied the ship to Haifa.

The refugees were prevented from disembarking in the port of Haifa. After armed resistance in which three Jews were killed, the passengers on the *Exodus 1947* were forcibly removed and taken to British ships waiting to return them to Europe. The refugees' plight and the extensive media coverage it generated became known as the "Exodus affair." It had a major impact on the post-Holocaust situation of the Jewish DPs, and ultimately on the decision of the British to leave Palestine and the subsequent establishment of the State of Israel.

Kaufman's last major assignment in Germany was to assess the needs of these *Exodus* refugees, who were returned to Germany on September 8, 1947. They were interned in special prison camps, and in these exceptionally tense conditions, Kaufman worked with the *Exodus*'s refugee passengers, particularly those in the camp at Poppendorf, where many of them stayed until they could immigrate to Palestine.

When Kaufman returned to the United States, bearing tokens of gratitude from the hundreds of people whose lives she affected, she resumed her career. She worked with Rabbi Mordecai Kaplan, the founder of Reconstructionist Judaism, and also advocated the study of the Hebrew language in the New York City public schools.

In "An American in Belsen," an article Vida Kaufman published in 1956, ten years after her service in Europe, she wrote: "For everywhere, the emphasis was on creating an atmosphere of living, living for the future and not in the past. . . . I treasure no title more than that which was given me in the camp—the American D.P."

Vida Kaufman

PORTRAIT OF ORKOW FAMILY

Portrait of Alex Orkow with his adoptive parents in Munich, Germany, December 1947. Gift of Alex Frank Orkow. When the atrocities of the Holocaust became known, Ruth and David Orkow decided to adopt child survivors. They adopted a son from a home for Jewish children funded by the American Jewish Joint Distribution Committee in Austria.

David and Ruth Orkow
Children of Their Own

He is getting lovable, learning to hug and kiss, and actually laughing. We had been afraid that he never would laugh, as I am certain that he did not for his first two years. Now he actually laughs with abandon like all the kids at home do who are loved and wanted."

So Ruth and David Orkow wrote home to their family and friends in America in their "Newsletter Number II" of January 1948. The lead article, indeed the only article, was the joyous description of their new baby, Alex, a two-year-old they had adopted from an orphanage in Austria.

When Ruth and David Orkow, a New York City couple unable to have children, learned of the enormous loss of Jewish life in the Holocaust, they decided to go to Europe to adopt two orphaned children. Although the outcome of the journey they launched themselves on in 1947 would turn out to be fulfilling and wonderful, the process would be anything but easy.

The Orkows were, by nature and choice of occupation, helpers: David Orkow was trained as a doctor and his wife as a teacher of homebound New York City children. They were well traveled, having been to Europe a half dozen times in the 1930s. They spent wartime years working as civilian employees of the United States Corps of Engineers in the Bahamas and later in Alaska. When they read about the organizing efforts to aid Holocaust survivors in Europe, the Orkows thought they would be ideal employees of the American Jewish Joint Distribution Committee (known as "the Joint"). The Joint was the American Jewish community's overseas relief and rehabilitation agency, which was then engaged in extensive work among the two hundred thousand Jews living in Displaced Persons (DP) camps in postwar Germany, Austria, and Italy.

The Orkows applied for positions with the Joint. During the interviews, they were also candid about their other primary objective: to go to Europe in order to

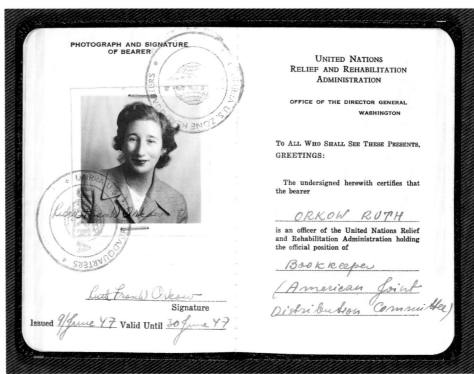

Certificates of identity issued to David and Ruth Orkow as staff members of the American Jewish Joint Distribution Committee by the United Nations Relief and Rehabilitation Administration. Washington, D.C., United States, circa 1947. Gift of Alex Frank Orkow.

locate orphaned children to bring back as their own to the United States. This struck a responsive chord with the Joint, and the Orkows went overseas in the summer of 1947. Both went to work in the American-occupied zone of Germany, Ruth in the financial department and her husband as the chief emigration officer for Bavaria.

The Orkows were having little success finding young, orphaned children. Almost no children under the age of six had survived the concentration camps. The young Jewish children who had survived the war—and who were now being brought from the DP camps and other locations to homes such as Burgl Gut children's home in Austria—had been hidden in Christian homes or in convents and monasteries; many had been hidden in the countryside by underground Jewish organizations.

By the fall of 1947, most of the children at Burgl Gut and other similar homes were over the age of ten. There were, however, some youngsters born to survivors who had died in the last months of the war or after liberation—or who were in circumstances so difficult that the child had to be given up. Alex Klein was one of these children. (To this day, nothing is known of Alex's life before Burgl Gut, except that those who left him there explicitly requested that he should never be told about his origins.)

Christmas Eve of 1947 found the Orkows at a party at the United States Army's Officers' Club in Munich. A social worker, who knew of their unsuccessful efforts to find young children, rushed up to them in great excitement. She knew of a two-year-old boy who was available at an orphanage near Salzburg! But they'd have to leave immediately and, after meeting the child, decide on the spot whether or not they wanted him. And their decision would have to be final; tomorrow all the children were being taken to Israel.

Optimistic, Ruth and David agreed that David would make the drive to Austria, while Ruth would return to their apartment to get it ready for the boy. David managed to arrange for a car and driver, and in the middle of a snowy December night, he crossed the border from Germany into Austria. The administrators of Burgl Gut who greeted David when he arrived in the wee hours of the morning awoke Alex and brought him to meet David.

"I've got to be crazy!" David thought, but "I'll take him" is what he said. So within minutes, Alex found himself turned over to a complete stranger, who bundled

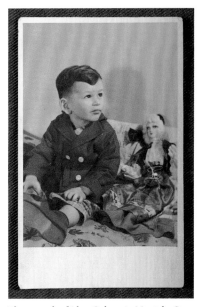

Photograph of Alex Orkow in Munich, Germany, shortly after his adoptive parents, David and Ruth Orkow, took him out of a home for Jewish children, 1947. Gift of Alex and Frank Orkow.

him into a car and drove off with him in the middle of the night. He was terrified. He began wailing; he soiled his pants; the air in the car got oppressive. As the car approached the border crossing, David thought, "How do I explain this? I've got a screaming child, no papers for him, and it's the middle of the night." The guards at the border crossing were the same U.S. soldiers who had passed him through only hours before. When David rolled down the window and they saw the bawling child and got a whiff of the air, they said, "You've got enough trouble!" and waved the car through.

Alex began his life with the Orkows in Munich. They assembled recommendations on their suitability as parents—including letters from the Joint—and the adoptions of Alex and a younger sister, whom they named Linda Ann, were completed. In Munich, the Orkows joyfully set up their new family, hiring cooks and nursemaids to assist them. "We needed a stroller (a Sportswagon) and since they are not to be had, Ruth traded one of her dresses for one, so that Alex can now be taken for a stroll and not have to be lugged about. He is too heavy to carry any longer." The children thrived and so did their parents. "You would not know me, as I have changed and everybody has told us both that we have become different and nicer."

Then a major setback. Although they were now adopted, the children were still subject to the United States immigration quotas and would not be allowed entry into the United States in the near future. David's position as a top immigration officer for the Joint allowed him to meet with congressional aides who were doing research for what would become the Displaced Persons Act of 1948. David explained their dilemma: How could they not bring their adopted children, who were also displaced persons, home to America? The aides said that they would see what could be done, and when the Displaced Persons Act of 1948 became law, Section 3 (b) provided that 3,000 "eligible displaced orphans may be issued special nonquota immigration visas. . . ." Alex and Linda Ann were issued visas number one and two. (Subsequent immigration acts extended this provision. Thus, the resolution of the special difficulties originally faced by the Orkows has made it significantly easier for thousands of children to become part of American families.)

The Orkows returned to New York in 1948, and the children continued to bring enormous joy and satisfaction into their lives. This was threatened, however, in the immediate years after their return, when Jewish welfare agencies began to question the Orkows about irregularities in the adoption procedures. When the Orkows sensed that there was a possibility their children might be taken away, they knew that whatever the "irregularities" were that had occurred under the frenzied postwar conditions, they could not allow Alex and Linda Ann to be uprooted again and certainly not from loving parents.

An attorney relative of the Orkows suggested that if they moved out of New York to the Midwest, the agencies there would be far more sympathetic to the family's concerns. As it turned out, within days David Orkow was offered a job in Omaha, Nebraska. Sensing the fates at work, the family soon relocated there. He became the director of the local Jewish home for the aged, and Ruth Orkow taught junior high school. Alex grew up to be an architect and businessman. His sister, Linda Ann, still lives in Omaha, Nebraska, where she has raised five sons.

MILITARY JACKET

Worn by Fay Rechtman in the Israel Defense Forces, adapted from a British uniform. Israel, May 1948. Gift of Fay Rechtman Storch. Rechtman arrived from New York in 1947 as an engineering student and joined the Haganah, the underground military force that merged into Israel's army in 1948.

Fay Rechtman Storch

"They had me stealing guns from the British. . . ."

Her rifle was Czech; her jacket was British; her cap, with its strange flap, was of unknown provenance; but her pants were from the Bronx. Fay Rechtman (also known as Zipora Yemini in Israel) wore a uniform that was indeed unorthodox, even ragtag. Yet her pride in it, as a member of the newly created Israel Defense Forces, fighting in the spring of 1948 for the establishment of the Jewish state, was enormous.

Fay Rechtman's journey to the land that was about to become the State of Israel began not in the Bronx, where she was born and raised, but in the Ukraine, where her father, Abraham Rechtman, growing up in the midst of intense anti-Semitism, first developed his Zionist ideals. Against the wishes of his Hasidic father, who counseled waiting for the Messiah, Abraham Rechtman followed his ardent Zionism to Palestine in 1910 to become an active participant in efforts to establish a Jewish state. After three years, he returned to the Ukraine and was reconciled with his father. After his father's death, from injuries sustained in a pogrom, and faced with conscription into the czar's army, Abraham Rechtman chose, instead, to walk across Siberia to China, through Japan, and from there, ultimately, to travel to the United States. There he met and married Bronia Zwick, who shared his strong Zionist convictions.

Fay Rechtman, born in 1926, the first of three children, inherited her parents' love of the Land of Israel. After high school, she entered the City College of New York to study electrical engineering. Because she was one of a handful of women among some five thousand male engineering students, life was difficult.

When the opportunity arose, Fay applied to and was accepted by the Technion, the engineering university that had been established in Haifa in 1912, in part through the assistance of the American philanthropist Jacob Schiff. When she ar-

Photograph of Fay Rechtman. Israel, circa 1948. Collection of the Storch Family.

rived in September 1947 to celebrate her twenty-first birthday in Haifa, she was also celebrating the fact that she had become the first American woman accepted for matriculation to this prestigious technical university.

Although she was doing well in school and enjoying her life, it was impossible to ignore the whirlwind of international politics and the immediate drama of the unfolding Zionist experience that had begun, specifically, three months before Rechtman's arrival. In May 1947, Great Britain was under intense pressure from all sides, particularly from the activities of the Haganah. The Haganah, the Jewish underground defense forces, had been struggling to bring in refugees, many of them concentration camp survivors, plus thousands of other Jewish immigrants, on illegal ships such as the *Exodus 1947*. The aim was to challenge British policy in Palestine and to galvanize the world's attention to the Jewish people's right to their own homeland.

Finally, on November 29, 1947, two thirds of the members of the General Assembly of the United Nations voted to adopt a plan that would partition Palestine and include the creation of a Jewish state. The Jews accepted the plan; the British said they would neither object to nor enforce it. However, surrounding Arab countries in effect declared war to destroy the Jewish state at birth. The War of Independence had begun.

The Technion was closed, and Fay Rechtman secretly joined the Haganah. Because she knew English, she found employment at British depots and offices. She helped to steal guns desperately needed by the Haganah, as the Jewish defense forces scrambled to defend all areas of the country against the Arab armies that were being assembled. With her American passport, Fay was able to pass through British checkpoints without being searched. She once actually hid a gun under her skirt as she went through a checkpoint. Trusted by the British, she was also able to steal letters containing intelligence, which she passed along to the Haganah.

During the first months of the War of Independence, the Haganah was forced into a defensive posture. In an Order of the Day issued by David Ben-Gurion, the prime minister of the Jewish provisional government, the Haganah became part of the Israel Defense Forces. On May 14, 1948, Ben-Gurion declared the creation of the State of Israel, and the United States gave de facto recognition. On the same day, Arab armies invaded, and heavy battles ensued.

Fay Rechtman now wore the uniform of the Israel Defense Forces (IDF). "There

Newspaper clipping of Fay Rechtman and two others on their way to Palestine, circa 1947. Gift of Fay Rechtman Storch.

IDENTITY CARD

No. 69860

Name of holder ZIPORA YEMINI

Place of residence HAIFA

Place of business HAIFA

Occupation STUDENT

Race JEWESS

Height 5 feet 9 inches

Colour of eyes BROWN

Colour of hair BROWN

Build TALL

Special peculiarities

Signature of issuing officer

Appointment

Office stamp partly over photograph.

Signature of holder

Place HAIFA Date 2.3.48

Government of Palestine identity card issued to Fay Rechtman. Haifa, Israel, 1948. Gift of Fay Rechtman Storch.

Fay Rechtman Storch

was so little time between the declaration of the United Nations and the British leaving, there wasn't time to equip an army," she remembered. "So we just grabbed whatever was around, bits and pieces. British, American, French, Czech." Pasted together as it was from various sources, her uniform was emblematic of the heroically improvised army that now faced large Arab forces. Fay worked in the intelligence department, developing photographs and also photographing and enlarging military documents brought in by agents. Fluent in four languages, she also helped in translation.

The fighting continued through the summer, as the army of the new state achieved many, if costly, military successes throughout the country. By January 1949, armistice agreements were being worked out, and a Jewish state was becoming a political reality.

In 1950, David Ben-Gurion and the new state's parliament, the Knesset, passed the Law of Return, providing for free and automatic citizenship for all Jews. As a Jew in Palestine when independence had been declared, Fay Rechtman was automatically a citizen if she so chose. She, however, decided to return home to the United States because of her mother's poor health. She settled back in the Bronx, married Milton Storch, and together they raised two children.

When the children were old enough, Fay Rechtman Storch enrolled part time in Columbia University as a linguistics major. In May of 1982, she graduated summa cum laude, Phi Beta Kappa.

155

PHOTOGRAPHS OF DEPORTED JEWS

Exhibit at the Museum of Jewish Heritage—A Living Memorial to the Holocaust of two thousand Jews deported from France. Photographs gathered by the Association of Sons and Daughters of Jews Deported from France and by Serge and Beate Klarsfeld in an effort to preserve the identities of Jews murdered in the Holocaust. Visitors to the Museum can look up the names and last known addresses of many of these individuals, as well as the number and date of the convoy on which they were deported to Auschwitz-Birkenau.

Serge Klarsfeld
Rescue the Dead

When Serge Klarsfeld and his wife, Beate, displayed the photos of six-year-old Ginette Cukier or twelve-year-old Jacques Friedmann or any of the twenty-five hundred children whose truncated lives and terrible deaths they were able to document, they allow the viewer to walk just a little bit into the children's lives. There—baguettes on the table, and in the corner the Hebrew primer left open on the chair; there's Paul Gobert's bar mitzvah service; and a grassy corner of the Bois du Boulogne, where Emile Messyngier and Jean Landau might have kicked the soccer ball watched by proud parents—you can hear the silly jokes they told, the love they felt, the dreams they had.

Yet because nearly all the children in the photographs were murdered by the Nazis—barely 300 of the 11,402 deported children survived—in doing this work of documentation, Klarsfeld often had an impulse both thrilling and painful: to rescue the dead.

> When you read about someone, you feel something inside yourself, you want to save him. You feel yourself no longer here today, but you are carried back by the research and the faces into 1942 or 1943. You want to shout to them! You want to tell them what is coming. You desperately want to help someone to survive. But then you realize this is your hope and your imagination at work, and you cannot save them from being killed. But you *can* save them from being killed once again by time and oblivion.

Serge Klarsfeld himself was almost one of these children. Born in Bucharest, Romania, Klarsfeld and his family, like many others escaping from the Nazis, had found temporary refuge in France. They had gone to Nice in September of 1942, in part because it was in the Italian zone of occupation, where the Italian army, with the support of senior government officials, prevented the arrest of Jews.

A year later, however, as the Germans occupied all of France, including Nice, the family became hunted again. On September 30, 1943, Alois Brunner, a key SS officer involved with the deportation of Jews from France, broke into the apartment building in Nice where the Klarsfelds lived. Serge found a place to hide behind a partition in the back of a closet. From here he heard the Germans breaking down doors, beating up his friends, and arresting them. From his concealment he heard his father shouting, "Help! Help! We're French. Save us!"

Having survived the war in yet another hiding place in the upper Loire Valley, Klarsfeld determined to find out precisely what had happened to his father. All he knew was that he had been taken to Auschwitz-Birkenau and killed there. Already a lawyer, with a sense of the importance of documentation and how one prepares a case, Serge went to Auschwitz, which, in 1966, was a place rarely visited by foreigners. He was on a kind of personal pilgrimage of memory to uncover every possible detail about his father.

Going through the archives of the numbers of prisoners at Furstengrabe, one of the labor subcamps of Auschwitz, where the prisoners were worked to death at coal mining, he found his father's number. Klarsfeld deduced that laboring at Furstengrabe must have been punishment exacted by the Nazis for an infraction committed by his father. Then, after six months of slave labor in the mines—the limit of what prisoners could endure—his father would have been deemed no longer useful. He would have been sent back by the German mining engineers to the SS for killing in the gas chambers at Auschwitz-Birkenau. Klarsfeld also found a document detailing the Gestapo's search for himself, his mother, and sister.

For the work he was about to begin, Klarsfeld had the help of his wife, Beate, a German Protestant and the daughter of a Wehrmacht soldier. She had lost her politically sensitive job by publicly questioning the Nazi pasts of prominent German politicians. Together, the Klarsfelds launched themselves on their lifelong campaign to document the victims of the Holocaust, particularly in France. Their meticulous historical research, ongoing advocacy in the world media, and refusal to see Jews as anonymous victims aided them in tracking down and successfully prosecuting Nazi officials in France.

Beate Klarsfeld led a relentless campaign beginning in 1971, when she ferreted out Klaus Barbie in Bolivia. Barbie had been the SS officer in the Lyons region. He had led the roundup of forty-four Jewish children who were given refuge in the small hamlet of Izieu, in central France, in spring 1944; all were killed. When Barbie was brought to justice in 1987, Serge Klarsfeld was one of the lawyers who successfully prosecuted him on behalf of the victims' families.

The Klarsfelds' historical and legal work led the way in France, shining an uncomfortable and uncompromising light of truth on French collaboration in the deaths of seventy-five thousand Jews of France, who were rounded up by French authorities and turned over to the Germans between 1942 and 1944. Serge and Beate Klarsfeld continue today to work for the extradition of Alois Brunner from Syria. They visit and speak out in Bosnia, Rwanda, and other places where new genocidal crimes have occurred.

From the Klarsfelds' book, *French Children of the Holocaust,* let us hear the voice of Jacques Friedmann, twelve years old when he was deported on convoy 55 of June 23, 1943, with his parents, two brothers, and three sisters. Before he died, he wrote a wry and dignified letter to a former teacher:

> Dear Sir:
>
> We have been in the camp of Limoges since 7 o'clock Friday morning. From here I thank you for all your exertions on my behalf. There are twenty-five of us here. The youngest of the condemned is four weeks old. I wonder what crime this baby can possibly have committed. . . . Now we are all going to be skinned. No one can say there's no equality in France. But we are not despondent; on the contrary, we feel more courageous than before. We remain faithful to our Jewish tradition: love thy neighbor as thy self. Please accept the deep respect of your Jewish pupil.
>
> Jacques Friedmann

The Jews in the Changing World of the Twentieth Century

David G. Marwell, Ph.D.,

with Igor Kotler and Yitzchak Mais

It is hard to imagine a century whose history affected a people more profoundly than the twentieth century affected the Jews. The fifth decade of that century saw not one but two transforming events—the Holocaust and the establishment of the State of Israel. At nearly midcentury, these events, like the waist of an hourglass, were a culmination and a beginning. In this narrow band of time, it was as if the enduring themes of all of Jewish history—exile, martyrdom, and renewal—were distilled and recapitulated.

In telling this history, the Museum of Jewish Heritage—A Living Memorial to the Holocaust remembers the tragedy of the Holocaust and celebrates the hope and values that have always characterized Jewish life. The three floors of the Museum seek to portray Jewish life in the twentieth century before, during, and after the Holocaust and thereby provide a crucial and often overlooked context to the darkest years in Jewish history. The artifacts and stories that we have included in this book mirror the spirit and approach of the exhibition. The Museum presents the human drama and highlights the personal narrative of individuals who actually experienced the historical events. In many history museums, artifacts are displayed to tell us about a particular event or time period rather than about the individuals who lived at that time. Both in the exhibit and in this collection of stories, we seek an intimacy with the historical "participants" and hope to create a powerful emotional experience to be remembered long after the facts, figures, and maps have faded.

Our visitors are given an opportunity to focus on themselves—their own backgrounds, traditions, and history—as they encounter the values, customs, and heritage of the Jewish people. The more universal a story is in its appeal, the more it can bridge cultural differences. The life experiences of any group are unique, but they reflect traits and emotions that are common to all people—hope, desire, frustration, fear, courage, survival, and triumph.

Throughout more than three millennia, the Jewish people settled in and then left behind, often by force, major centers of civilization. The center of Jewish life moved from Canaan to Egypt, Israel, Judah, Babylonia, Spain, Germany, and Poland. By the beginning of the twentieth century, although Jews lived throughout the world, with large communities in Germany, Austria-Hungary, Great Britain, Romania, North Africa, and the Middle East, almost half of the Jews lived under the rule of the Russian czars. A great migration, which began in the 1880s, was under way. Hundreds of thousands of eastern European Jews migrated to the United States, making it, first demographically and then culturally, one of the most important centers of Jewish life.

Jews entered the twentieth century as a remarkably diverse people. They lived in countries in every part of the globe. They were Ashkenazi and Sephardi, capitalists and communists, secularists and traditionalists, nationalists and assimilationists, Zionists and Bundists. They were individuals committed to life in their native country, and they were those who chose to emigrate. Some spoke the languages of home and community—Yiddish, Hebrew, Ladino, Judeo-Arabic—others spoke the language of the native country. They were remarkably different and yet remained linked by common roots, shared practices, and communal values. The new century challenged this community, bringing with it burning issues and problems from within and without.

The rise of nationalism in Europe and the development of nation-states introduced powerful new ideas of nationality, ethnicity, and, ultimately, race. The old definition of the Jew, based on religious observance, could not be applied to a new class of Jewish nonbelievers who did not give up their Jewish identity. A modern phenomenon, Jewish nationalism, came into being. Zionism, coalescing into a political movement in 1897, offered secularists a Jewish national identity. Alongside this development, some Jewish socialists and communists, who rejected the longing for a Jewish homeland, supported the idea of a Jewish national or ethnic identity. At the same time, those who hated Jews found new ways to express and rationalize their anti-Semitism.

The emancipation of the Jews, which gave them legal equality as citizens, starting with the French Revolution, led to new developments within Jewish communities and for individual Jews. Ideas of democracy spread in western Europe and North America contributed significantly to the change of the status of Jews. Before World War I, Jews in the United States and western Europe had established themselves in the intellectual and business elite of society. It was not rare to find scientists, scholars, writers, artists, or composers among the Jews of the West. A significant number of non-Jews in the West accepted Jews as equals, apparent in the growing number of Jewish civil servants, elected officials, and political leaders and in the rise in mixed marriages.

The experience of the Jews in eastern Europe was less successful. In czarist Russia, Jews were officially second-class citizens, limited in their right to vote and to hold office, as well as in their rights of settlement, education, and occupation. Their history was punctuated with tragic events. In 1903, there was a pogrom—a violent attack against Jews—in Kishinev, followed by a wave of pogroms in 1905 and 1906. In 1911 in Kiev, a blood libel, an accusation that Jews murdered gentiles to obtain their blood for ritual purposes, violently disrupted life for the Jews. Poverty and oppression drove some politically active Jews to become Zionists or revolutionaries, while many immigrated to the United States, Canada, and other democratic countries.

World War I ushered in a period of significant change. At the end of 1917, the British government published the Balfour Declaration, which declared in favor of the establishment of a national home in Palestine for the Jewish people. Although Jews had to wait another thirty years until their dream was fulfilled, the Balfour Declaration and the ensuing transfer of Palestine to mandatory status under British supervision allowed Jews to establish several offices in Palestine, including the National Council, which would form a kernel of the future government. The Jews of Palestine also created the first Jewish military units of the modern era.

The Communist revolution in Russia in 1917 and the defeat of Germany and Austria-Hungary in World War I led to the split of Russian Jewry. A significant minority (roughly 40 percent) became subjects of the Soviet regime, while the majority of the Jews found themselves in independent Poland, where they were granted the status of a national minority. Consequently, after 1918, Poland, where the Jews made up 10 percent of the total population, became the major center of Jewish life.

The variety of Jewish life and culture in Poland in the interwar period was striking. Along the political spectrum, Jews were found in the Agudath Israel, an ultra-Orthodox religious party, on the one side, and in the Bund, a party of Jewish Marxists, on the other. The Zionist movement encompassed all socioeconomic factions of Jewish society—religious, secular, liberal, bourgeois, socialist, capitalist, et cetera. Hasidism flourished along with secular Yiddish culture. Many Jews lived in shtetls, with almost exclusively Jewish populations, and others gravitated to large cities. In Warsaw, for example, Jews accounted for one-third of the population. Organized systems of Jewish education provided religious and secular teaching in Hebrew and Yiddish. Towering Jewish writers and poets, such as Israel Joseph Singer, Itzik Manger, and Avrom Sutzkever, along with countless Jewish scholars, lived and worked in Poland. The 3.3 million Jews of Poland were the backbone of the Jewish people and the primary source of Jewish cultural and religious creativity, making them the center of Jewish life on the eve of World War II.

In the meantime, the United States had gained strength as a dynamic center for Jews. Two and a half million Jews made their way to the United States between 1880 and 1924. While they brought many old customs to the New World, many modified or abandoned their traditions in order to Americanize themselves. In America, a large group of eastern European newcomers came into contact with a much smaller, but very influential, group of German Jews and their descendants, who introduced them to the Reform movement of Judaism. The newcomers enjoyed the spirit of freedom and opportunity in the United States. Along with economic developments, American Jewry established a multitude of communal and educational institutions, whose drive and energy made the American Jewish community a vital center of Jewish life, with a population of more than 5 million by 1939.

The third major Jewish population, numbering almost 3 million, found itself under Bolshevik control in the Soviet Union—citizens of a country that had declared war on religion. Within two decades, the number of synagogues in the Soviet Union was reduced by a factor of seven; heders were banned; yeshivas, with a few exceptions, were closed; and atheism was promoted to the rank of government policy. This war on religion led to the rapid secularization of the Jews of the Soviet Union.

The Jewish population of Palestine, known as the Yishuv, although numerically small (about 500,000 persons or about 3.5 percent of the world Jewish population by 1939), was pivotal in Jewish history. Within the Yishuv, the first Jewish agricultural settlements were founded, including the kibbutz, the radical experiment in utopian community. These communities, as well as towns under Jewish management with Hebrew-speaking populations, were part of a great cultural renaissance. Moreover, the first Jewish secular institution of higher learning, the Hebrew University, was established in Jerusalem in 1925.

By 1933, Jews in Europe and North America enjoyed, if not equality, significant opportunities. Jewish politicians occupied important posts in France, Germany, Great Britain, and the United States. The Jewish tradition of education and the new opportunities available in a democratic society brought spectacular results: between the wars, a larger percentage of Jews attended universities than that of any other ethnic or national group. Jews, now more accepted and with new perspectives gained through education, made their mark in modern pursuits, as represented by such giants as Albert Einstein, Sigmund Freud, Franz Kafka, Sergey Eisenstein, and Marc Chagall.

In 1933, Adolf Hitler came to power in Germany, the home of the largest Jewish community in western Europe, numbering approximately 550,000—less than 1 percent of Germany's total population. Step by step, the Nazi government turned Jews into outcasts in their own country, a country in which they had lived for more than a thousand years. The Nazis saw history as a struggle of races, in which the Germans, who formed the "Aryan" race, were forced to protect themselves against inferior peoples, the Jews chief among them. Specific laws were promulgated based on concepts of "racial hygiene," including those that made sexual relations between gentile Germans and Jews a crime. Systematically, and with the veneer of legality, Jews were excluded from German life. Ostracized socially, banned from the civil service and other forms of employment, prevented from studying, and excluded from positions of status, Jews were victims of a concerted, if at first bloodless, attack on their ability to lead normal lives. They were encouraged at first to leave Germany, abandoning their property and wealth, to seek refuge in a world that increasingly restricted the absorption of immigrants.

All too frequently, Jews under Nazi domination have been viewed as mere objects in a reign of ongoing tragedy and terror, and have been characterized as passive victims of persecution. This perspective minimizes the many Jewish responses and initiatives that were undertaken in the face of isolation and persecution, and ignores the continued resourcefulness and vitality that Jews exhibited within the limitations imposed by the calamity and crisis that they experienced.

German Jews struggled to lead normal lives in an abnormal situation. Uncertain about their future, and believing, like others throughout the world, that the Nazis were a passing phenomenon, they focused on coping with daily hardships. For example, they created the Kulturbund, the Jewish Cultural Association, to offer barred Jewish artists the opportunity to perform with newly organized orchestras and theaters throughout Germany. Jewish doctors, lawyers, teachers, athletes, and others excluded by the Nazis from their professions established resourceful alternatives. By January 1937, half of Germany's sixteen hundred Jewish communities were dissolved or were on the verge of disappearance, as rural Jews sought safety in the cities. Increased economic hardships required the Jewish community to provide extensive welfare services.

These diverse activities reflected the Jewish community's sense of solidarity and cohesiveness, as well as its collective will to resist an increasingly hostile environment. Moreover, through these efforts, Jews hoped to confront the crisis and to "ride out the storm" by sustaining themselves both spiritually and materially.

Prewar Nazi policy turned bloody and culminated in Kristallnacht, a pogrom that took place in November 1938, during which synagogues throughout Germany were destroyed, Jewish shops and businesses were plundered, and thousands of Jews were arrested and imprisoned. Many were beaten, killed, and driven to suicide. Tens of thousands of terrified German Jews fled the country.

Only with the beginning of the war did the Nazis unleash the full measure of brutality that was the logical extension and fulfillment of their hatred for the Jews. When Poland fell into Nazi hands in 1939, its 3.3 million Jews, with approximately 2 million under Nazi domination and the remainder in the Soviet-occupied area of Poland, had no place to flee. To isolate them from the rest of the Polish population, the Nazis set up ghettos, where the Jews were held under guard pending a more permanent solution to the "Jewish problem." Jews suffered from hunger, disease, and overcrowding. The Nazis often banned educational institutions, public worship, and cultural activities. Jews were doomed to a fate of slow death.

Although one of the major objectives of the Nazi administration in the ghettos was to dehumanize them, Jews found ways to organize their lives and to develop religious, cultural, and social activities banned by the Nazis. The carrying out of seemingly basic tasks, such as education for children or worship for the pious, became filled with new and urgent meaning and were an often overlooked form of Jewish resistance. In spite of the overwhelming odds against them and the difficulty of fully comprehending the unprecedented threat that confronted them, some Jews were also able to engage in armed resistance. They joined partisan units and rose up against the Germans in some ghettos and camps, most notably in the Warsaw Ghetto in 1943.

The Nazis ultimately developed a plan for the total extermination of the Jewish people: the "Final Solution of the Jewish Question in Europe." This monstrous effort was meticulous, calculated, and well organized. The destruction of Jews became one of the major imperatives of German policy, requiring organization, planning, and material resources coordinated by a special office within the SS and police authority. Special units, or *Einsatzgruppen*, were formed as a part of the SS and police. These mobile killing squads operated in the Soviet Union and Baltic countries after the German-Soviet war broke out in June 1941. Often following in the footsteps of the combat troops, they shot more than a million Jews near their homes. Shooting, however, was not considered efficient enough, and the Nazis developed new, technologically advanced methods of mass killing. Gassing was selected as the most productive method and the one that had the perceived benefit of placing less psychological stress upon the perpetrators themselves.

Poland, the major reservoir of the Jews, was chosen as the location for a series of extermination camps: established in December 1941, Chelmno was the first, followed by Belzec, Sobibor, and Treblinka. The concentration camps at Auschwitz and Majdanek had mass-killing facilities installed, and Auschwitz-Birkenau became the largest of all the Nazi death factories. Victims were exploited for their labor, their belongings, and even the value of their bodies. Nazi doctors performed horrific "medical" experiments on their prisoners, corpses were robbed of gold teeth and fillings to augment the Reich treasury, women's hair was woven into fabric for insulation and other purposes, and human ashes were strewn on the fields as fertilizer.

To carry out a task as enormous as the total destruction of the European Jews required the collaboration of the local populations. From France to the Soviet Union, and from Norway to Greece, the Nazis were successful in recruiting local collaborators. Some joined local police units, while others betrayed their Jewish neighbors. In the Baltic states and throughout the Soviet Union, locals served in killing squads and as camp guards. Without the cooperation of existing government bureaucracies and agencies, the Nazis could not have achieved their goals in Western Europe.

Of course, there were the few who helped Jews to survive. Motivated by humanistic, political, or religious principles, many risked their own lives to save Jews. The ranks of those who helped and rescued Jews ranged from single individuals to whole villages and, in the case of Denmark, an entire country. Thousands of Jewish lives were saved by rescue activities and operations. The majority of Europeans, however, were neither collaborators nor rescuers, but rather bystanders. They observed the persecution of Jews from the sidelines, some with satisfaction, some with pity, and many with no particular feeling at all.

The Holocaust had a profound effect on world Jewry. More than 30 percent of the Jewish population was lost, dropping from 17 to 11 million, with more than half of the 6 million victims being Orthodox Jews. Many Hasidic dynasties were wiped out completely. Famous yeshivas were destroyed. Even Jewish material culture and monuments were targets of the Nazis and their collaborators: synagogues, Jewish cemeteries, and entire Jewish neighborhoods were razed. Nazism gave an almost mortal blow to Yiddish and Yiddish culture. The shtetl became history. The old Polish center was destroyed, while other old European Jewish centers suffered profoundly. Jewish Vienna, Jewish Prague, Jewish Vilna, and Jewish Salonika were no more.

Surviving Jews were faced with an almost unthinkable challenge: to rebuild their lives in the face of near total destruction. For most, there was no place to return to. They had lost family, friends, homes, and possessions. Some lost faith in their fellow humans, and some lost faith in God. That many were able to bring themselves back to live productive lives must surely be one of the most inspiring stories to emerge from this darkest history. That the Jewish birthrate in the Displaced Persons camps, which became homes to many surviving Jews, reached epic levels was an indication that Jews were determined to rebuild.

In 1948, in the shadow of the Holocaust, the Jewish people experienced one more transformational event—the establishment of the State of Israel. By the early 1950s, the massive influx of new immigrants made Israel the third largest Jewish community after the United States and the Soviet Union. With nearly 2 million Jews, it became a crucial center for Jewish life.

The history of Israel is often related as the history of Arab-Israeli wars. Indeed, the short history of Israel is punctuated with defining military events, the most far-reaching being the Six Day War in 1967. Each decade has seen existential struggles that have changed the map of the land and the hearts and minds of its people. Undoubtedly, these wars affected Israeli society and world Jewry in significant ways, but the history of Israel is equally one of construction—political, economic, cultural, and intellectual. Much had to be started from scratch; even the Hebrew language had to be adapted to modern times. The land had to be made fruitful, and diverse immigrants from more than one hundred countries, speaking seventy languages, had to be fused into one nation. Towns and agricultural settlements had to be provided with a modern infrastructure. Democracy had to be established and developed.

World War II and the Holocaust also transformed American Jewry. The destruction of the European center turned the United States into a major focus of Jewish life. The American Jewish community was the largest in the world: American Jews felt themselves an integral part of American society without giving up their Jewish identity, religion, and culture. As a result of their unique position, Jews in the United States made spectacular progress in society, playing a role in all areas of intellectual, economic, and political life.

With the establishment of Israel and the emigration of Jews from Eastern European and Muslim countries, the majority of Jews lived in democratic societies. Still, until the fall of communism, every fifth Jew resided in a communist country. In 1971, the Soviet Union opened its gates for many Jews who dreamed of going to Israel or the West. In the 1970s, more than 160,000 Soviet Jews settled in Israel and more than 70,000 moved to the United States, other English-speaking countries, and Germany. After a new stage of emigration from the Soviet Union, which began in 1987, many hundreds of thousands of Soviet Jews migrated primarily to Israel and the West. The Russian-speaking community became the largest ethnic group in Israel, numbering almost a million persons. About 300,000 to 400,000

Soviet Jews settled in the United States and represented up to 10 percent of Jews in large urban centers. In Europe, the German Jewish community became the fastest growing in the world, and the only one in the West in which Soviet Jews make up the majority.

The twentieth century saw the destruction of the old European Jewish centers and the decline of Jewish communities in Muslim lands. Two new major centers of Jewish life emerged in Israel and the United States. The changed Jewish globe also included a newly invigorated geographic diversity in South Africa, Australia, Canada, and South America. Perhaps the most striking phenomenon in the Jewish world was the emergence from powerlessness. The ability of a Jewish state, along with Jewish communities worldwide, to protect Jewish interests is undoubtedly a unique development in the post-Holocaust era.

In a broad view of Jewish history, the twentieth century can be compared in impact to the period following the destruction of the Second Temple. By that time, Jews had lost the last remnants of their statehood. The destruction of the temple and the ensuing Roman persecutions led to huge losses among the Jews and the near complete dispersion of the Jewish people. Jewish life was transformed in every way—religiously, politically, socially, and economically. Over the centuries that followed, Jews were transformed from agriculturists to urbanites, from the people of the land to the people of the diaspora. The destruction of the temple led to significant changes in religious practice as Judaism entered its rabbinic period. Jerusalem was destroyed.

Twentieth-century transformations were similar in scale and import. The Jews experienced enormous losses in the Holocaust. Their religion was modified with the development and growth of the Reform and Conservative movements and with the emergence of women as leaders, and there was considerable secularization. But, in a reverse process of sorts, some Jews began to speak Hebrew again and a Jewish state was born. Many Jews became agriculturists in the new Jewish state. As Jerusalem returned to Jewish hands, the diaspora shrank, and today more than 5 million Jews make their homes in the State of Israel.

These transformations also dramatically changed our world. The Holocaust and the establishment of Israel were watershed events in the history of Western civilization. The Holocaust, in all its dimensions, challenged all previously accepted notions of human nature. The rebuilding and renewal of life and community after the Holocaust, including the creation of the Jewish state, an event that altered how Jews perceive themselves and are perceived, reaffirmed the vitality of the Jewish people. The compelling stories in this book tell a part of this history as they memorialize the unprecedented tragedy of the Holocaust and celebrate the continuity of Jewish life.

The Jews in the Changing World of the Twentieth Century

Acknowledgments

As a staunchly devoted volunteer Gallery Educator, Sally Magid spends a good deal of time in the Museum's galleries engaging visitors. Here, she encounters again and again the need that visitors to the Museum have to be able to hold some of these poignant memories in their hands. It was in response to that need that she and her husband, Abe, generously provided funding for this publication. We are indebted to them for their gracious gift, which allows these stories of memory and hope to be shared with our visitors and friends.

Director David Marwell's essay concisely places the 36 individual stories into a broader historical narrative, giving them the context that could not have been developed in the shorter essays. While he in no way intends this to be a comprehensive picture, he has undertaken to surround the personal histories with the global ones. He was skillfully assisted by the Museum's senior historian Igor Kotler. The 36 stories themselves were crafted by writer Allan Appel, who used to greatest advantage the unique quality of the survivors' and witnesses' own voices. We thank Elaine Freed Lindenblatt for her substantial contributions to the article "Aryeh Steinberger: Sukkah of the Lion."

The Board of Trustees, leadership, and staff of the Museum have made it possible to develop this project in all its richness. Dr. David Altshuler, founding director of the Museum of Jewish Heritage—A Living Memorial to the Holocaust, conceived of the project, provided inspiration, and saw it through its early phases.

Dr. Ilana Abramovitch managed the project with her usual spirit, holding these fragile memories with both hands and nurturing them into the compilation you have before you. Tracy Figueroa diligently coordinated the countless details of the project and kept the whole team on schedule.

We are indebted to the hard work and support of the Department of Collections and Exhibitions, led by director Dr. Louis D. Levine. We are especially grateful to archivist Bonnie Gurewitsch, registrar Jamie Hardis, assistant registrar Lindsay Artwick, and preparator Matthew Peverly. We are also thankful for the assistance of librarian Dr. Julia Bock. We are grateful for the insights and enthusiasm of director of communications Abby Spilka, and assistant to the director Rina

Goldberg. We extend thanks to Michael Stafford and Frank Camporeale in the operations department for their dexterity and good humor.

Yitzchak Mais, former chief curator of the Museum, was an essential part of the team that put together this book. We would have been hard pressed to do it without him.

A number of Museum volunteers and interns willingly helped with translations, transcriptions, and research: we appreciate the contributions of John Bradman, Philipp Bulgarini, Emina Hadzic, Bertha Lowitt, Renata Singer, Michael Spielholz, and Shirley Weiner.

A project as complicated as the production of this volume would not be possible without dedicated interns who worked energetically without complaint. They include Jeremy Kadden, Tamar Kaplan-Marans, Amelia Klein, and Aurélie Segal. We are especially thankful to interns Lauren Israel and Kate Weiss for their diligent fact-checking work during the summer of 2001.

At Bulfinch Press, Michael Sand, our editor, energetically supported this major publication project of the Museum. We also appreciate the contributions of designer Jerry Kelly, editorial coordinator Sarah Chaffee, and senior contracts associate Barbara Nelson.

We are grateful to Richard Goodbody, who did all the new photography for the book. His beautiful photographs capture the poignant personal qualities of the artifacts. We acknowledge David Finn, who donated his photography of the magnificent Steinberger sukkah. We would also like to acknowledge Peter Goldberg for additional photography and Mike Joyce of Platinum Design for his design of the cover.

We are also grateful for the unflagging and enthusiastic support of Karen Gantz Zahler, our literary agent, and the staff at Weil, Gotshal & Manges LLP, especially Robert Sugarman and Bernadette McCann-Ezring.

The book you hold in your hands would not have been possible without the generosity of the people who donated or loaned artifacts and shared their families' stories with the Museum. By doing so, they created the very reason for this volume's existence. Our great appreciation goes to:

Association of Sons and Daughters of Jews Deported from France; John Balan; Joseph A. and Dorothy Frank Bamberger; Louis Bannet and Ken Shuldman; Denise Feiler Bensaid; Carol Biermann; Frania Bratt Blum; Toby Blum-Dobkin;

To Life:
36 Stories of Memory and Hope

Sonya Trachtenberg Breidbart; Henry Coleman; Ludwig Ehrenreich, Zachary Ehrenreich, and Margaret E. Heching; Robert, Kornelia, Thomas, and Kate Ehrlich; Shlomo Farber; Paulette Feiler Goldstein; Eli E. and I. Marilyn Hertz; Bernard D. and Hilda Fischman; Judith Naomi Fish; Joan E. Gerstler; Gerald and Cynthia Granston; Hannah Storch Keller; Serge and Beate Klarsfeld; Samuel Klapholz; Edna Klinovsky and Batya Nachum; Leo Baeck Institute, New York; Arnold H. and Mary Levinsky; Celia Levinsky; Jehuda, George, Robert, and Paul Lindenblatt, sons of Jeno and Piroska Lindenblatt; Rabbi David Lipman; Allen Magid; Jerome and Carolyn Mahrer; Peretz and Blanche Milbauer; Henry Morley; Alex Frank Orkow; Simon and Chaya Palevsky; Joseph L. Pessah; Elizabeth, Gail, and Sandy Peters; Rabbi W. Gunther and Elizabeth S. Plaut; Richard Rozen; Shirley Schulder; Rose Skier; Judith Steel; Abraham Stein; Stanley Stern; Milton and Fay Rechtman Storch; Elizabeth Kroó Teitelbaum; Magda Tewner; Herbert von Peci; Andor Platschek Weiss; Irene White; Moses Zupnik; Yaffa Eliach Collection (Center for Holocaust Studies); YIVO Institute for Jewish Research.

Ivy L. Barsky
Deputy Director for Programs

INDEX

Never forget. There is hope for your f...

זכור לא תשכר לאחריתך תקוה צ

esperansa para tu postremeria. Akod

דיין צוקונפט גע דענק... קיין מאל

Remember... Never forget. There is

תקוה לאחריתך זכור לא תשכח

... Hay esperansa para tu postremeria

פא צו ניט מאל קיין גע דענק... גע דענק פא

be for your future. Remember... New

זכור לא... תשכח יש תקוה לאחו

... Nunka te olvides. Hay esperans...

אל ניט צו פארגעסן פאראן לאפא

forget. There is hope for your future.

תשכח יש תקוה לאחריתך זכור...

Akodrate... Nunka te ol...